JOURNEY FOR JUSTICE

Journey
for
Justice

How "Project Angel" Cracked
The Candace Derksen Case

MIKE MCINTYRE

GREAT PLAINS
PUBLICATIONS

Great Plains Publications
345-955 Portage Avenue
Winnipeg, MB R3G 0P9
www.greatplains.mb.ca

Great Plains Publications gratefully acknowledges the financial
support provided for its publishing program by the Government
of Canada through the Canada Book Fund; the Canada
Council for the Arts; the Province of Manitoba through the
Book Publishing Tax Credit and the Book Publisher Marketing
Assistance Program; and the Manitoba Arts Council.

Design & typography by Relish Design Studio Inc.
Printed in Canada by Friesens

FIRST EDITION

Library and Archives Canada Cataloguing in Publication

McIntyre, Mike
    Journey for justice : how "Project Angel" cracked the
Candace Derksen case / Mike McIntyre.

ISBN 978-1-926531-13-7

    1. Derksen, Candace, d. 1984. 2. Grant, Mark Edward.
3. Murder--Manitoba--Winnipeg. 4. Murder--Investigation--
Manitoba--Winnipeg. I. Title.

HV6535.C33W55 2011   364.152'309712743   C2011-904697-0

ENVIRONMENTAL BENEFITS STATEMENT

Great Plains Publications saved the following
resources by printing the pages of this book on
chlorine free paper made with 40% post-consumer
waste.

TREES	WATER	ENERGY	SOLID WASTE	GREENHOUSE GASES
8	1,403	6	536	1,827
FULLY GROWN	GALLONS	MILLION BTUs	POUNDS	POUNDS

Environmental impact estimates were made using the Environmental Paper Network
Paper Calculator. For more information visit www.papercalculator.org.

INTRODUCTION

I will never forget the day a community's desperate search for a missing girl came to a tragic end.

It was January 17, 1985—my 10th birthday.

I didn't know Candace Derksen, but like a lot of Winnipeggers, I felt like I did. As a naturally curious child, growing up in a neighbourhood not very far from where Candace lived, the story of the 13-year-old girl who mysteriously disappeared while walking home from school had captivated me.

And frightened me.

Looking back, the case was probably one of the first times I realized that the world we live in isn't always a happy or safe place. Sadly, I know a lot of kids learn this lesson in a much more direct and tragic way, but I credit my parents for raising me in a nurturing environment where I always felt protected.

As the years passed, I often though about Candace—especially as each birthday would come and go. I wondered whether her death would ever be solved, whether her family and friends and loved ones would ever get the answers they so desperately wanted and needed.

Those feelings grew stronger as my journalism career began in 1995 and I got to know members of the Derksen family, specifically Candace's parents Wilma and Cliff. They are two of the strongest, most courageous people I know and my heart always ached for their loss.

And so I naturally felt a sense of relief for them when police emerged in 2007 with an astonishing announcement—they had made an arrest in one of the country's most notorious cold case mysteries.

A lot of Canadians have followed this case closely, and it was with great pride that I found myself covering a story which I always felt such a strong connection to.

It's a bond I was once again reminded of when the following email arrived in my inbox from Wilma Derksen on January 17th, 2011.

"Dear Mike. If I remember correctly this is a special day for you. Hope you are surrounded by love. Wilma."

It was a touching gesture from a grieving mother who was just hours away from facing her daughter's accused killer in court as his high-profile trial was set to begin.

And so it is with great honour, and responsibility, that I embraced the idea of writing a book about the Candace Derksen case. This is my fifth book, and it was the most personal and painful to write.

There are so many people to thank, with Cliff and Wilma and their amazing family at the very top of the list. Their support and encouragement of this project was a true blessing. They also introduced me to their remarkable support network, which includes wonderful family members, friends, neighbours and more who have helped them not only survive, but thrive.

Wilma also graciously allowed me to excerpt small portions of her own book, *Have You Seen Candace*, which provides readers with a unique voice and insight into the frantic days and weeks following her daughter's disappearance. Those excerpts in *Journey For Justice* appear at the start of a handful of chapters in italicized form. Other content in Wilma's book helped me form an important foundation for some of the early days of this story, including specific dialogue and key events.

I strongly encourage everyone to purchase a copy of Wilma's book, which was first published in 1991, and tells the kind of personal story only a mother could capture. Her blog, at www.wilmaderksen.blogspot.com, is also a must-read and is updated regularly.

Everything you will read in *Journey For Justice* is based on first-hand interviews with the subjects, sworn testimony, court documents, exhibits filed during the trial, parole documents and a litany of previously published newspaper stories and columns spanning more than 25 years, along with information contained in *Have You Seen Candace*. No dialogue has been improvised, assumed or re-created. Any conversations are a result of direct recollection for at least one of the involved parties.

Special thanks to Aimee Fortier, the Executive Assistant to the Chief Justices and Chief Judge of the Manitoba Court of Queen's Bench who also works as the media relations officer for the courts and judiciary in Manitoba. She helped facilitate my access to some of the above documents.

I would wish to thank my own family for their love, understanding, and enthusiasm for this project. My parents, Ted and Susan, wife, Chassity, and our two children, Parker and Isabella, are a constant reminder of what is truly most important in life. I am forever grateful and thankful for their presence and patience.

Finally, I would like to dedicate this book to all who have lost a loved one. Let the Candace Derksen story be a reminder to never give up hope, to cherish each day and to never become so consumed by the past that you forget to live in the present.

Life is a journey. Make the most of yours. Embrace it. Don't waste it.

—MIKE MCINTYRE
www.mikeoncrime.com

PART ONE

1

TUESDAY MAY 15, 2007

They strolled through Winnipeg's downtown core, armed with brooms and clad in bright orange and yellow vests. Bright smiles were visible on all four faces as they stopped on the sidewalk outside the MTS Centre, the city's newly-constructed professional hockey arena. This was their moment in the sun.

A popular Canadian evangelical Christian TV station was in town to film a feature story on a local job-training program. They would be the feature attractions.

All four had been accepted into the program through Siloam Mission, a charitable shelter and soup kitchen. The goal of Mission: Off The Street was quite simple—teach members how to follow basic scheduling and routines, such as showing up for work on time, to develop valuable skills needed for employment.

The work was equally basic—sweep and clean downtown streets. They would show up at the shelter each day at about 9 a.m. for breakfast, participate in daily devotions and then spend the next three to four hours sweeping streets.

A female reporter from *100 Huntley Street* gathered the group into a half-circle, microphone in hand, as the camera began to roll. Each participant briefly introduced themselves by first name.

"Mark," said the man on the far left.

The gaunt, grey-haired man was wearing baggy, faded blue jeans, a bright blue t-shirt and a wide smile that displayed several missing top teeth. He proudly discussed being accepted into the job-training program about a month earlier.

"I was out of work, I was on welfare," said Mark. "Welfare doesn't pay enough money to get us going, to make ends meet."

The reporter asked how he'd been enjoying his first few weeks on the job.

"It's better than sitting at home doing nothing. It gives me some pride, you know, it gives me some self-esteem," said Mark. "All of us here are fighting different addictions, you know. Some are drugs users, some are whatever. We're all just trying to survive the best we can, make a life."

The reporter turned her attention to the other three in the group for similar introductions.

Sonny was a young aboriginal man who admitted he's been struggling with various addictions throughout his life. He was now trying to upgrade his skills, having only completed grade 8.

"This keeps me occupied, keeps me out troubles, away from my addictions. It's pretty difficult to stay away from that stuff. I'm doing myself a good deed. Am doing the city a good deed," he said.

Sandy was a middle-aged Caucasian woman who was lucky to even be standing here. She'd been living on the streets, collecting welfare, when she was run over by a car. Sandy was now trying to piece her life together, which included kicking a nasty cocaine habit.

"I couldn't get any help. I have a hotel room now, am trying to work so I can move into an apartment building," she said. Sandy was also hoping to reconnect with her five grown children.

Rick was a middle-aged Caucasian man who spoke in a whisper as he described trying to get back on his feet and land full-time employment. Like the others, addiction was holding him back.

Mark interjected, taking it upon himself to speak for the group. "I wish people would really try to understand why these people are there," he began. "Some of it's because of their own choosing. Some of them are mentally ill. Some of them don't have pride, some of them don't have self-esteem, some of them don't have an education. Some of them come from the richest families in the world but they end up on the street because their heart's been broken or their pride or they're looking for something or searching or trying to find their way where they belong in life and where they belong on the streets, you know, they're just trying to fit in."

Mark gave scant details about his own background, yet appeared to the *100 Huntley Street* reporter to be quite passionate about their subject.

"We're not bad people," he continued. "Some of the best people in the world are the street people. You know, you get to know them, you get to know the heart, you get to know what they're about. They're not all just looking for money, some of them are legit, some of them do buy food with their money that they get. There is the odd one that will buy a drink or whatever, you know, just to calm down or whatever, to relax, but most of them when they beg money they need it for a good reason. You know, they need it for diapers or whatever, like the young girls today."

Mark said he found it nearly impossible to survive on the limited funds of welfare, and many others had similar difficulties. "Some people only get $80 a month on welfare. How are you going to survive on that? You can't. The food banks are more busier than ever, and because of that, you know, people are just learning how to get on and find a way to survive," he said.

The reporter wrapped up the interview by asking everyone in the group what their ultimate dream was.

Rick described wanting to be able to buy new clothes one day, rather than always wearing hand-me-downs and donated garb.

Sandy wanted some good health and a stronger relationship with family.

Sonny had his eyes on a big prize. "I'm gonna get rich one of these days," he said with a smirk, explaining how he uses much of his pay to buy regular lottery tickets.

Mark finished the interview by describing a much more basic goal. "I'm not looking for a pot of gold or a million dollars," he said. "I just want a meal every day, you know, take care of myself, make sure I eat. I'm just trying to survive."

Unfortunately for Mark, the documentary would never be aired. But he would soon be thrust into the national spotlight for a much different reason. He was the prime suspect in one of the country's most notorious cold cases, enjoying his very last day of freedom.

2

It was one of those ordinary days that should have slipped obliviously into November's row of days like all the other days of that month, like all the other days of all the other months of that year. Sometimes we may wish we remembered our days more clearly, more vividly, but it might be a blessing that we don't. I will never forget what happened that day, and there are times I wish that I could.

....

FRIDAY NOVEMBER 30, 1984

Wilma Derksen surveyed the family room and wondered when the hurricane had blown through. And why cleaning always seemed like a case of one step forward, two or three steps back?

It was already mid-afternoon of what had been an extremely hectic day filled with grocery shopping, laundry, paying the bills and finishing off some last-minute writing assignments.

Her 13-year-old daughter, Candace, would be home from school shortly. She could hear nine-year-old Odia and three-year-old Syras playing upstairs, likely creating yet another mess to clean up. Actually, playing was probably not the right word. It sounded like an argument had erupted.

Wilma stopped her scurrying for a moment to listen, wondering whether this sibling dispute would quickly resolve itself or if she needed to play the worn-out role of referee and head upstairs.

It seemed cooler heads had prevailed. Wilma silently thanked the cartoons they were watching for coming back from commercial and turned her attention back to the disaster zone that was the basement. She picked up a rotting apple core from behind the television, reminding herself to scold Candace for that little gift. She plucked a toy motorcycle from the couch cushions and told herself to give Syras the usual speech about putting his toys away.

She grabbed scraps of paper that were strewn all over the floor, the product of Odia's obsession with origami. Although she admired her daughter's artistic talents, Wilma wished she'd put as effort into cleaning up as she did in her handiwork.

Wilma recognized she had contributed to the clutter as well. A stack of *Reader's Digest* magazines were not in their proper place, nor were several papers and slides she had left lying around.

Wilma anxiously glanced at the clock, knowing time was her enemy on this day. They were having company, and the newly-cleaned family room would soon be filled with two giggling teenagers.

Candace was having her good friend Heidi Harms come the following morning for a weekend sleepover. Wilma paused for a brief moment to soak in the temporary sounds of silence, knowing the next 48 hours would be jam-packed with activity. She knew she'd spend much of the weekend driving Candace and Heidi around the city. The girls were planning on hitting the malls, along with maybe some swimming and skating if the weather was nice.

Wilma figured she might be able to take advantage of the time out of the home to get some much-needed Christmas shopping done. She had nearly finished tidying the basement when the telephone rang.

"Mom," the voice said on the other end of the line.

It was Candace.

....

She had just picked up the telephone to call her mother when David Wiebe approached with his icy surprise. Seconds later, Candace was wiping the snow from her face, revealing a huge smile.

"David just gave me a face wash, Mom," Candace giggled.

"David?" Wilma replied, a hint of concern in her voice. She had been hearing the name a lot lately. Any enthusiasm for her daughter's apparent crush had been tempered by the fact David was a full two years older than Candace.

It had only been a few weeks ago that Candace came home from a school music event at the downtown Winnipeg Convention Centre, seemingly walking on air.

"Mom, he's crazy," Candace said, blushing. She repeated that several times throughout the night.

Wilma had expressed some concern, privately, to her husband. She asked Cliff to "check him out" with Lily Loewen, the outdoor education director at Camp Arnes. Candace and David had both attended the Christian camp, which is located about 100 kilometres north of Winnipeg on Lake Winnipeg, the previous summer. Candace had worked the horses while David was involved in a leadership training program. Wilma knew that Lily went to the same church as the Wiebes and could surely deliver the goods on David.

Cliff had come back with a positive report—David was a good kid, from a real nice family. Still, Wilma's protective motherly instincts continued to take over. She repeated her concerns once again while on the phone with her daughter, who was still laughing at what David had just done to her.

"Careful now," Wilma said.

"Oh, Mom," groaned Candace.

Wilma realized it was almost 4 p.m. Cleaning up the house had consumed more time than she thought.

"I thought you'd be on your way home by now," Wilma told her daughter.

Candace was calling from Mennonite Brethren Collegiate Institute—MBCI for short—which was the Christian middle and secondary school she attended.

"Aw, Mom. It's Friday. Can you pick me up?" Candace replied.

This wasn't an uncommon request, and Wilma normally obliged. In fact, she had originally planned to drive her daughter home from school but had let the afternoon get away from her. But now, this late in the day and with more housework still to be done…

"Mom, someone is waiting for the phone," Candace said impatiently, still somewhat out of breath and giggling from the schoolyard shenanigans with David.

Wilma dreaded the prospect of getting Odia and Syras bundled up and out of the home.

"Candace, this is bad timing. If you had called sooner, maybe we could have gone shopping with the kids before picking up Daddy. But right now I'm in the middle of cleaning the family room for you and Heidi and the kids are cranky. If I pack them into their snowsuits it means waiting in the car. Can you take the bus?" said Wilma.

There was a pang of regret to her response, but Candace clearly understood. "Sure, it's okay," she said.

Wilma knew it was unseasonably warm outside, the temperature only a few degrees below zero Celsius. There had been little snow so far in November, but everyone knew this wouldn't last. In fact, the forecast called for much colder temperatures on the weekend. Still, she felt bad.

"Look, if Dad can get off early, I'll pick you up. I'll call him. Call me back in five minutes," said Wilma. "And don't flirt too much!"

Candace laughed before hanging up. David had another ball of snow in his hand and aimed directly at his smiling target.

It was a mutual crush between the two school friends, although David was somewhat hesitant about it. It wasn't just the two-year age difference. It was also the fact they were four grades apart. David had skipped a grade, while Candace had been held back a year.

"Where you going?" David asked Candace after she'd cleared away the remnants of his latest face-washing.

"I'm just going home," she replied.

"Too bad, if I had my licence I'd drive you home," David said. "If I didn't have Drivers Ed I'd walk you home."

"It's OK. I live close by," said Candace. In fact, it was only about a 15-minute walk home, which didn't seem like such a big deal on a nice day.

David and Candace exchanged one final set of mischievous smiles before she exited the school parking lot and headed home.

....

Wilma knew right away this wasn't going to work.

"I can't, I'm busy. Pick me up at five," Cliff Derksen said into the phone. Wilma had just called, wondering if this was one of those occasional Fridays when he could finish up early. His quick, somewhat curt response told her otherwise. Now she was scrambling for a solution. If she picked up Candace now, they'd all have to sit around in the family's lone vehicle for at least 30 minutes waiting for Cliff to finish work.

Odia and Syras had finally calmed down enough to stop arguing with each other. But she knew it wouldn't last long, and both kids were likely getting hungry. Candace would be ravenous as well. The prospect of any kind of time spent inside a parked car with three cranky, starving kids was not appealing.

It was decided. Candace would either take the bus home or walk, and then Wilma would take all three kids to grab Cliff at 5 p.m. They would then go to McDonald's for a quick bite to eat to get their weekend started.

Wilma would then drop Cliff, Odia and Syras at home while taking Candace shopping for some weekend treats to share with Heidi, just as she'd promised her daughter earlier that day. Wilma knew Candace would understand.

The phone rang again.

"Mom?" said Candace.

"Candace, do you have money for the bus?" Wilma asked.

"Yup," said Candace. In fact, Candace had already started walking home, stopping now at the Redi Mart convenience store on Talbot Avenue to use the phone following her initial conversation with her mother.

"Okay, I can't pick you up now, but tonight we can go shopping alone. Is that okay?" said Wilma.

"Yup, see you," said Candace.

She hung up.

Candace thanked the store clerk for allowing her to use the phone before walking out the front door to continue home.

....

Wilma raced with the housework, hoping to get everything done in time for Candace's return home. She finished vacuuming the basement and quickly folded a bit of laundry. The family room looked great, although Wilma figured Candace might want to move a few things around before Heidi arrived the next morning.

Wilma was lost in her thoughts, still fretting about not being able to drive Candace home. She wondered why it was bothering her so much. Wilma suddenly jolted. Both physically and mentally.

She was immediately consumed by a feeling of dread.

3

The clock on the wall suggested Candace should have already been home. The feeling in the pit of Wilma's stomach suggested something was wrong.

"We have to pick up Candace and Daddy," Wilma told Odia, and Syras. They had been consumed by a cartoon on television and hadn't noticed the urgency with which she'd just entered the room.

Wilma cast a nervous glance out the front window of her Herbert Avenue home. She was stunned at how quickly the weather had changed. The ground was now covered in snow, a stark change from just two hours earlier when Wilma had been outside to pick her son up from a babysitter.

It had just started snowing when she'd walked in the door at 2:30 p.m., but the flakes were large and fluffy and melting as soon as they hit the ground. Now, they were much smaller and staying exactly where they fell. And the sky was growing darker by the minute.

Wilma paced the main floor of the house, going from the front window to the kitchen for a look out the back alley. It was getting close to 5 p.m. Candace knew they had to leave to pick up Cliff, so surely she wouldn't have stopped somewhere on her way home. She had also left for school that morning wearing just a thin polyester blouse underneath her coat. The plunging temperature outside would no doubt have hastened her pace home.

Odia and Syras were taking their sweet time getting dressed, oblivious to the concerns of their mother. Wilma ushered them out the front door and into the car.

"Odia. Keep your eyes on your side of the road, and I'll watch mine," Wilma instructed her nine-year-old.

"I've got good eyes, Mom. Right?" said Odia.

Wilma planned to drive the exact route Candace normally took home, figuring she'd spot her daughter socializing with a friend on the sidewalk. She drove slowly down the back lane first, and then turned on Talbot Avenue to be greeted by a swarm of rush-hour traffic. She passed by the neighbourhood 7-Eleven store, carefully gazing inside to see if Candace was there. Nothing.

The further she drove, the faster her heart began to pound.

"Mom, where is she?" Odia asked, now a hint of concern in her voice for the first time.

They had reached Mennonite Brethren Collegiate, Candace's school. And there was still no sign of her.

"I don't know," Wilma answered, attempting to keep her voice as calm as possible. "Why don't you check the school doors?"

Odia hopped out of the car, approached the doors and gave them a pull. They were locked. The schoolyard was empty as darkness had now set in and the snow continued to fall. Wilma's mind was racing. She debated whether to turn back and continue to drive the same route, or go pick up her husband as planned.

Wilma felt like she needed Cliff to be with her right now. She turned her car towards Henderson Highway, parked in the back and walked into the Camp Arnes office. She wanted a private moment with her husband.

"I can't find Candace, Cliff. I'm worried," Wilma said as soon as she got within earshot. She filled him in on what had occurred. The initial phone call from school, the second call a few minutes later. The frantic drive to the school.

"Cliff, nothing would keep Candace from coming home from school today. Heidi is coming. She wouldn't do anything to jeopardize this weekend," said Wilma. "Cliff, I'm scared, I think this is serious."

Wilma immediately sensed her husband's concern. He didn't have to say a word. In 15 years of marriage you learn to read a person pretty well. And Cliff was an open book right now.

Now back in their vehicle, Wilma suggested they go back down Talbot Avenue. She would watch the left side, Cliff the right. They told Odia to keep an eye on both sides. Syras sat quietly. The street was still packed with cars but void of any pedestrians. It had become bitterly cold, the kind of weather nobody wants to get caught outside walking in.

Wilma wanted to go back to the house, figuring Candace had maybe taken a different route home. She had even left the doors unlocked just in case.

The car had barely come to a stop in the driveway before Wilma was out the door and into the house. Cliff was left behind to get Syras out of his seat.

"Candace," Wilma shouted upon opening the door.

"Candace," she yelled again, now into the basement.

"Candace," Wilma repeated a third time while running upstairs.

There was no response. The house was quiet. Wilma returned to the main floor, where Cliff was now helping both kids out of their winter clothing.

"Cliff, where is she?" Wilma pleaded.

"Tell me again how she sounded on the phone. Was she upset that you didn't pick her up?" asked Cliff. "Does she have money with her? Could she have met a friend on the way home?"

Wilma raced back upstairs, checking the dresser drawer in Candace's room. The money she had been saving up for her weekend visit with Heidi was still there.

Cliff was already putting his jacket back on when Wilma returned.

"I'll drive back to the school. We might have just missed her," he said.

"I'll call her friends," Wilma replied.

She walked over to the television, turning it on for Odia and Syras, hoping it would provide enough of a distraction. But she sensed Odia was now tuning into the panic she was feeling.

Wilma began working through a list of telephone numbers Candace had written down only months earlier.

Wilma had asked her two daughters to compile a friend list in case of emergencies. She hadn't imagined having to actually use it one day.

Deanna was first on the list; she was a close friend of Candace's who had known her since elementary school. Wilma knew Deanna was a natural leader among her peers. If anyone knew where Candace had ended up, it would likely be Deanna.

Wilma's initial optimism was quickly shot down. Deanna had no idea where Candace had gone.

"I can call around for you, though," the teen offered.

Wilma began poring through the list. She was struck by how many names she didn't recognize. It was as stark an indication as any of how much her daughter was growing up, how the switch from elementary school to junior high school had affected her.

Candace had always been a social girl and had no difficulties making new friends. Cliff and Wilma had decided to send her to MBCI hoping to she could make some new Mennonite friends, believing it would make her life easier.

It had been that way for Wilma, who grew up in a fairly strict household in which things like movies, school dances and most certainly makeup were forbidden. For Wilma, her parents' rules were easier to digest when she had friends growing up in a similar environment.

Cliff and Wilma also hoped that Candace would discover her spiritual side at MBCI. To them, good values and morals and an understanding of God and the Bible were just as important as a solid education. They believed MBCI would be a perfect fit. The school of more than 400 students was well-established in Winnipeg.

Candace had initially balked at attending the private school when many of her elementary friends were going to Elmwood High School. So they had struck a deal, one they intended to honour—give Grade 7 a try, and if you're still unhappy at the end of the year, you can switch to Elmwood for Grade 8.

Any doubts Candace may have had were quickly erased. Wilma recalled fondly how she picked her daughter up one day in September, about a week into the new year, and Candace had a big smile on her face. "You were right, Mom. They're my kind of people," Candace had said.

Her grades had been decent, not spectacular, but that had nothing to do with intellect. Candace was as smart as they came and could do anything she put her mind to. But to her, school was often seen as just a place to hang out and socialize with friends. And her marks sometimes suffered because of it.

Wilma was quickly moving through the list without any success. Every friend who answered hadn't seen Candace since the school day ended. Wilma was able to cobble together a few details of what happened in the moments preceding her daughter's call for a ride home.

Her friends spoke of her packing up her gym clothes from her locker to take home to wash, of heading out of the school wearing her burgundy backpack, of using the telephone to call Wilma, of the playful snowball fight with David Wiebe.

And of leaving the school grounds, headed for home. Alone.

....

Wilma heard the door open. It was Cliff, his face showing an obvious expression of concern.

"Is she home?" he asked.

Wilma shook her head.

"Any word?" he asked.

Another negative shake.

Wilma explained her various phone calls to Candace's friends and their lack of information. They sat in silence for a few minutes, staring blankly at each other.

"Let's call the police," Cliff said abruptly.

Wilma paused. "Not yet," she said. "There's one person I still want to speak to … David."

Wilma had never met David Wiebe but had heard plenty about him from Candace. She told Cliff about the face wash he'd given their daughter while on the phone.

"Do you think she's with him?" asked Cliff.

Wilma said she didn't think that was the case. But she wanted to see David, face-to-face, to get a better feel for what might have happened.

"I'll feed the kids," Cliff offered.

....

It was now close to 7 p.m., a full three hours since Wilma had last spoken to her daughter. She drove slowly from her home to MBCI, checking in every direction to make sure Candace wasn't walking by.

The sidewalks were bare.

Wilma was mentally preparing for her meeting with David, recalling several previous incidents Candace had spoken about. She remembered jokingly asking her daughter recently if she might be in "love" with David.

"Mom, don't be silly. He's in eleventh grade," she had replied, giggling.

Wilma arrived at the school and found a hub of evening activity. This included choir practice which she knew David would be attending. She quickly found the principal, Harry Wall, and explained why she was there. He pointed out David Wiebe, who was standing near his locker.

"You must be David," Wilma said upon approaching him.

She was exactly as she'd envisioned—a handsome looking boy with fair hair and a sparkle in his eyes. He was the type of boy Candace would have immediately fallen for, a carbon copy of all the other boys she'd had crushes on going all the way back to Grade 1.

"I'm Candace's mother. Candace hasn't come home from school today. She mentioned that you were with her after school. Do you know where she is?" asked Wilma. Her tone was anxious, but not accusatory in any way.

David's face immediately showed a look of concern. "I thought she was going home," he said.

"Was that after the face wash?" asked Wilma. "She told me on the phone that you gave her a face wash with snow."

David flashed a quick smile. "Actually, I gave her two. One before she called you and another one before she went out," he said, pausing briefly. "Mrs. Derksen, the last time I saw her she was walking down Talbot in the direction of your home. I had driver's training after that so I didn't hang around ... this is serious, isn't it?"

Wilma could sense his sincerity and concern.

"I'm so sorry," David continued, putting a comforting hand on her shoulder. "I'm sure she'll show up."

Wilma was fighting back tears. She quickly thanked David and turned away, heading out of the school and back to her car. She had no doubt David was being truthful and didn't know where Candace was. And she felt a sense of utter hopelessness that the best bet for locating her daughter had come up empty.

"No, God! No!" Wilma screamed upon returning to her vehicle. She slammed her fist on the steering wheel.

"No! Not my Candace!"

4

*Somewhere I once read that it is often when peo-
ple are in crisis that they throw their faith away—
at the very time when they need it the most. I had
read that and wondered idly how I would react in
a crisis. I didn't know. I don't think any of us know
what we are going to do in advance. The last time I
had been in what I perceived to be a life-and-death
crisis, I hadn't thrown my faith away, but I certainly had rethought and revised it afterward. The crisis revealed that my faith wasn't based on reality
and that it needed to be revamped. But since that
time, my life had been routine: a domestic scramble to make ends meet. As I faced this new crisis, I
wondered vaguely if my revamped faith would hold.
Was it based on reality this time? Would it give me
strength? Would it give me direction? Or would I,
after all of this, have to rethink it again, revise it, or
throw it away? I knew I was about to find out.*

....

It was a typically busy Friday night in Winnipeg for members of the city's police service. The late-afternoon snow
may have scuttled the social plans of some, but it hadn't
slowed down the usual surge in calls associated with the
start of a weekend.

Police officers were already busy dealing with the expected assortment of drunken disputes, domestic strife and car accidents, which had spiked tonight because of the slippery road conditions. It was just after 7:30 p.m. when the call came in about a missing teenage girl.

"Are you sure she isn't with friends," the female desk officer responded to the father on the other end of the line.

Cliff Derksen was taken aback by the question. He had picked up the phone the second his wife had walked through the door with nothing to report from her trip to Candace's school and chat with David Wiebe.

"Yes, we're very sure. We've checked with all her friends," Cliff said in a calm, controlled voice that masked what he was feeling.

"We are absolutely certain she isn't with friends. We've checked everyone and everything. We're up against a wall. Something is wrong," Cliff added.

The police officer didn't seem convinced.

"Was she upset?" she asked.

"No, she wasn't upset," Cliff replied. "She was look-ing forward to having her best friend come to our place. They were going to spend the weekend together."

Wilma stood by her husband's side, nodding in agreement.

"Her best friend lives in Arnes, 50 miles away from here. They haven't seen each other in weeks. I know she wouldn't have run away today," he continued.

There was temporary silence on the phone.

"Look, if she isn't home in half an hour, we'll put this out to the Transcona fleet. Can you give me a description," she said.

Cliff gave the officer the basics—five-foot-one, about one hundred and five pounds, blue eyes, light brown hair—then turned to Wilma for clarification about what Candace had been wearing.

"Black wool jacket with burgundy raglan sleeves, tight blue jeans, and runners that are never tied. She was carrying a burgundy backpack, and she had black gloves," Wilma mouthed to her husband, who repeated her answer into the phone.

As Cliff finished up with the officer, Wilma retreated downstairs. She went straight for the boxes of photographs which had been piling up, just waiting to be put into albums. She began rummaging through the stack, looking for a recent picture of Candace. She suspected police would need one as soon as possible. The exercise took Wilma on an emotional trip down memory lane, her eyes fixed on several snapshots showing a smiling, happy-go-lucky Candace at various stages in her childhood. Yet none of the images seemed to portray the Candace of today, a rapid maturing young woman who was quickly approaching the cusp of adulthood.

Wilma returned upstairs with a handful of photos, which she spread out on the dining room table. Cliff was back on the phone with police, telling the same officer how the past 30 minutes had produced no additional developments. He was assured a missing person notice would soon go out to all officers in the area. The officer said she would call back in two hours for an update.

....

Odia and Syras had been perfect angels on this night, perhaps both picking up on the seriousness of the situation. But now it was time for bed, something Cliff and Wilma were dreading. They calmly assured their two children that everything was going to be fine.

"I promise that tomorrow, when Candace is home, we can do all the fun things we didn't get to do tonight," Wilma said.

Both children seemed to believe her. They fell asleep quickly, a relief to both Cliff and Wilma. Now what?

Time was now their enemy, every passing moment bringing more feelings of dread about where Candace could be. Cliff suggested he go for a quick walk through the neighbourhood, believing it was important to get a street-level view of things. He bundled up and headed out the door.

Wilma was left alone with her thoughts. And the pile of pictures on her table.

....

It was 9:30 p.m. when Cliff was back on the phone with police, the desperation in his voice becoming clearer. His walk to MBCI and back had yielded nothing but frozen frustration and fear.

Wilma stood by listening to her husband now pleading with police that there was nothing typical or ordinary about Candace's disappearance. His exasperation suggested he was fighting a losing battle.

Feeling helpless and useless, Wilma headed back downstairs. Her efforts from earlier in the day to clean the family room for Candace and Heidi's weekend sleepover had now been diminished by her mad scramble through boxes of photographs. She began tidying, convincing herself that Candace would soon be home and their original plans would be proceeding.

Cliff soon joined her, explaining how police had just expanded the missing person bulletin to the entire fleet of officers throughout the city. As well, police would be coming by their home around 11 p.m. to pick up a photograph of Candace and ask a few questions. There was a mutual feeling of relief, albeit temporary.

"There's still time for me to walk the school once more," Cliff said as they both headed back upstairs.

Wilma glanced at the outdoor thermometer on their kitchen window. Her heart sank. "It's so cold, Cliff. The temperature is still dropping. What if she's outside? She wasn't dressed for this weather," said Wilma.

"She won't be," Cliff replied.

Wilma wasn't sure how to take that. "Well, then what are you looking for?" she asked.

Cliff just shrugged his shoulders, a look of sadness on full display. "I don't know … tracks, anything that looks suspicious. I'll check the stores. I don't even know what to look for. I've just got to go," he said.

Wilma understood. She wished she could join him, but knew she must remain in the home for Odia and Syras. And to stay by the phone. She escorted her husband to the front door, shutting the door behind him as he stepped out into the darkness.

....

The two Winnipeg police officers arrived at their door, as expected, just after 11 p.m. Cliff had just returned home, another frigid, fruitless search of the neighbourhood completed. Wilma had the picture of Candace ready to go.

The couple expected a quick visit, believing the two officers would simply take the picture and head back out into the night to continue what they hoped was a massive search underway for their daughter. How wrong they both were.

The two officers accepted an invitation to sit at the dining room table, which was still covered with various photos of Candace. Cliff and Wilma both spoke at a frantic pace, explaining the last seven hours in panicked detail. The two officers sat there, taking a few notes, but spending much of the time just looking at Cliff and Wilma. Studying them.

It wasn't long before the questions began.

What kind of girl was Candace? What kind of parents were Cliff and Wilma? How often did they argue with their daughter? Had something upset her?

Both Cliff and Wilma were taken aback. They struggled to find the right words to explain the situation, to convey the seriousness of what they both knew had happened.

Cliff mentioned how he worked for Camp Arnes, the largest Christian camp in Manitoba. About how he'd previously worked as a pastor in North Battleford,

Saskatchewan. About the emphasis they placed on solid values, morals and family.

Neither officer appeared to be very convinced. They explained how abductions were extremely rare in Winnipeg, suggesting the last one was nearly a decade old. But they mentioned how there were as many as 100 runaway teens on the streets of Winnipeg at any given time, all by choice.

The officers said this sounded like a classic case of a frustrated teenager who decided she needed some time and space to let loose and run wild.

"I know what the problem is," one of the officers said.

"What?" Cliff said, exasperated at where this conversation appeared to be headed.

"You," he said in a commanding voice, staring directly at Cliff and Wilma.

"What do you mean?" asked Wilma, bracing for the reply.

"You're both religious, and Candace is rebelling," he said matter-of-factly.

They both should have seen this coming. Of course they would be pegged as overbearing religious fanatics, especially after Cliff mentioned his background.

Although their approach wasn't exactly delicate, the officers weren't asking anything Cliff and Wilma hadn't already silently asked themselves. Only to quickly dismiss. Wilma knew this wasn't the time for argument or debate.

"Okay, maybe you're right. But you know what teenagers are like, how important friends are to them.

Candace is expecting her best friend, whom she hasn't seen for weeks, to spend the weekend with her. They planned this weekend a month ago, and she hasn't talked about anything else since. No kid would run away if their best friend was coming the next morning. You're used to looking for motives? Well, the motivating force in Candace's life this weekend was to come home and get ready for her friend," said Wilma.

Wilma believed she had steered the wayward conversation back on track.

"Is she religious?" the officer said.

"Who, Candace?" asked Wilma.

"No, her friend," he said.

Wilma calmly explained that Heidi went to church, believed in God and was just like Candace—an ordinary Christian girl with a simple faith that was anything but fanatical. And it was true. Candace still enjoyed all the perks of being a teenage girl, including rock music, gossiping about boys and keeping up with the latest fashions.

"Are Heidi's parents religious?" the officer said, refusing to be driven away from his theory. "You see, this proves my point. Maybe Candace is rebelling against your whole religious community, and so she is rebelling against Heidi, too," he continued.

Wilma had never heard anything so ridiculous.

"No," Cliff interjected.

Wilma picked up a photo of Candace and Heidi, sitting underneath a tree with big smiles on their faces. "Look at them," she pleaded with the two officers. "You can tell even from this picture that they are kindred spirits. Even though they only spend the summers together, their friendship survives the long winters apart."

The painful back-and-forth continued for several more minutes. Police asked a few questions about Candace's marks in school and whether they had family outside of Winnipeg.

Wilma explained how the bulk of her family lived in British Columbia, while Cliff had relatives in Saskatchewan. Yet they insisted Candace would not be travelling anywhere, noting her modest pile of money was still in her bedroom dresser.

The two officers finally stood up to leave, taking Candace's picture with them and promising it would be distributed to police around the city. Cliff and Wilma thanked them, not entirely convinced the police believed anything they had said. Still, this was their only lifeline right now, one they weren't about to jeopardize in any way.

The officers promised to follow-up with updates as their investigation progressed. Cliff and Wilma felt like their nightmare was only just beginning.

....

Wilma sunk into a chair, feeling as down and depressed as she ever had. Yet Cliff seemed to have gained a second wind, somehow buoyed with new ideas as a result of the police interrogation. Despite the late hour, he picked up the phone and began calling the families of a few of Candace's friends.

It wasn't long before Cliff had a new tidbit of information—Candace had apparently spoken with the school guidance counsellor earlier that day. The news actually lifted Wilma's spirits. Could it be possible that Candace really *was* upset about something and was just blowing off some steam? Cliff wasn't going to wait to find out.

Dave Teigrob was asleep when the telephone rang and his wife picked up. The urgency in Cliff Derksen's voice quickly jolted him awake.

Teigrob was stunned to hear Candace was missing. He explained to Cliff how he'd spoken with her briefly earlier that day, but not about any issues or problems. And certainly nothing about any trouble at home. Teigrob quickly got dressed and headed over to the Derksen residence.

"I couldn't go back to sleep," Teigrob explained as Cliff and Wilma Derksen greeted him at their front door. It was midnight.

Cliff and Wilma had jumped at the sound of their doorbell ringing, briefly imagining opening the door to find their dear Candace standing there.

Their disappointment was quickly erased by the sight of a friendly, comforting face. Teigrob sat down with Cliff and Wilma, peppering them with questions in a much less hostile and suggestive way than the two police officers had.

Teigrob was as puzzled as they were, saying Candace appeared happy and excited about her future during their conversation in school.

He stayed with them until about 2 a.m., repeatedly offering words of assurance that Candace was likely off the streets, in a warm place and coming home soon. Cliff and Wilma were trying really hard to believe that was the case. But it was becoming increasingly difficult as the clock continued to tick.

Once Teigrob left, Cliff suggested they try to get a few hours of sleep so they could be refreshed in the morning. Wilma joined him in bed, but never closed her eyes. Cliff tossed and turned but was soon asleep. Wilma got up out of bed, walked into the living room and flicked on the porch light. She also unlocked the doors.

Wilma grabbed a chair and sat down, turning it so she had a direct view out of the front window. As she stared out the frosty front window, her eyes following every passing car, one question continued to consume her.

Finally, she asked it out loud.

"Why, God? Why?"

....

It was now 5:30 a.m. Wilma's eyes were heavy. A passing police car, with its lights and sirens, had provided a fleeting sense of hope that maybe there had been a development. She had briefly turned her eyes to the telephone, staring at it, expecting it to ring. Yet it didn't, a sure sign the emergency involved someone else.

Wilma had spent the hours praying quietly, asking God to be with her daughter at this critical time. To bring her warmth and comfort. To protect her from pain. For the first time, the reality began to hit her that Candace might already be dead.

Wilma was now feeling the cold despite sitting inside her home. Several blankets wouldn't stop the shivering. Raising the thermostat didn't either. She decided to join her husband, hoping the warmth of their bed would help.

It didn't.

She lay silently beside Cliff, who was still asleep. The stillness and silence of the room was overwhelming.

5

I sat up in bed. It could mean only one thing. 'Candace!' my soul shrieked. 'Are you in heaven?' Somehow the heavens were still open, and her presence seemed to fill the room. She was close, but yet so far—just out of reach. I wanted to enter fully into the next dimension, to ask her if she was okay, to ask her who had taken her away; but a soft, black velvet curtain fell between us and shut me out. She was gone. I couldn't penetrate the wall again no matter how hard I tried. But she was safe, I told myself over and over again. It was over. Whatever had happened was over. I closed my tired eyes, and the room went black.

....

SATURDAY DECEMBER 1, 1984

"She's not home?"

Wilma Derksen heard her husband's question mere seconds after their alarm clock began ringing. It was 6 a.m. Wilma couldn't find the words to answer.

"She could be at a friend's place," Cliff added, his voice nearly a whisper.

Wilma began crying. Moments later, when her eyes had started to dry, she began explaining the moment of clarity she'd experienced only a few hours earlier.

How she'd felt Candace's presence—only to feel it slip away.

"Then, it's all over?" Cliff asked.

"I can't say for certain. It's all feelings," said Wilma.

Tears began flowing from Cliff. Then again from Wilma.

"What do we do now? Do we continue to look for Candace?" asked Wilma.

"How certain are you? Do you have any doubts?" Cliff replied.

Wilma paused before answering. She didn't know what to think at this point. It had certainly felt real to her, as clear a sign as any that their daughter was gone forever. And yet, perhaps this was all just a product of her imagination. She was terrified, panicked and deprived of sleep. Those weren't typically the ingredients of clear, level-headed thinking.

"Can you tell me without a doubt that it didn't happen?" Cliff continued.

Wilma shook her head, indicating she couldn't.

"Do you believe me?" she asked.

"Yes. You obviously experienced something," Cliff said.

"But what do we do now?" said Wilma.

"We carry on," Cliff replied. "We look for Candace. We aren't 100 percent sure that Candace is dead, so we can't ignore the possibility that she might still be alive and need us. But we can keep the knowledge that probably she is safe in heaven as an inner comfort. Maybe we'll need it. Maybe God knows we will need it."

Cliff reached over and embraced his wife. "I wonder what must lie ahead of us that will make the knowledge of her death a comfort?" he asked quietly.

....

The new hours were filled with routine events which felt anything but. Get dressed. Wake Odia and Syras. Make sure they are fed. Make the beds. Do the dishes. Tidy up. Rinse and repeat.

Yet this was a Saturday unlike any other.

Cliff and Wilma delicately explained to their children that Candace still wasn't home, without giving any real indication of the worst-case scenario they both feared. Both knew they had to put on a strong front.

"This is serious, Odia," Wilma told her daughter in a private conversation later that morning. "We're going to do everything possible to find her. You can help us by looking after Syras."

The phone began ringing as news spread to family members and friends about what was happening.

The first call was from Dave Loewen, Cliff's boss and the director of Camp Arnes. He immediately sprung into action. "You need a search party. You need a lawyer. I'll make some calls," he said. There was absolutely no hesitation in his voice.

Dave Teigrob, Candace's school counsellor, called a short time later for an update.

Wilma called her parents in British Columbia. Cliff touched base with police. They began keeping a list of incoming and outgoing phone calls on a note pad next to their telephone.

It was mid-morning when the same two police officers who'd visited their home the previous night were back at their door. They had no update, but remained convinced Candace had likely just run away. One of the officers even discussed his own familial situation, describing how he was stunned when his teenage daughter once took off.

This was of absolutely no use or comfort to Cliff and Wilma, but they listened and nodded politely.

Police asked to look at Candace's bedroom. Wilma took one of the officers upstairs. Wilma found a series of notepads Candace had been using as a personal diary. She handed them over to the officer without request or any hesitation. He began reading the first few pages, and then abruptly laid them back down on a table.

"See, she did have problems," he said.

Wilma had been expecting this and was ready with an answer. She had never said Candace didn't have any problems. Doesn't every teenager at some point feel like their world is closing in? But Wilma explained that Candace's difficulties were no different than any other typical teen. And they were certainly not the type which would drive her away from the family and home she loved.

The officer didn't appear to be convinced.

"This girl's in trouble," he said.

Wilma couldn't believe it. As he was continuing to read one notepad, she picked up another and began leafing through the pages.

She quickly stopped on a poem she found, written by Candace.

Dear Lord. Thank you for getting me through the day. Thank you for my friends, for my Mom and Dad, for Odia and Syras, for food and for your support. Help my grandmas and grandpas and relatives and all the new babies. Give me the strength for the days and nights to come. Help me in my basketball games and my practices. And now I close with a clean heart, I pray.

Wilma couldn't suppress the smile. But it was quickly wiped away.

"You shouldn't be reading her diary," the officer said, grabbing the notepad away from her.

"I want to see if there is anything in here, a clue that will help us find her," Wilma replied, stunned at the officer's accusatory tone.

"A mother should never read her daughter's diary," he continued.

"Normally, I wouldn't. But she has shown this to me before, and nothing like that matters now. We have to find her," said Wilma.

"How will you explain it to her when she comes back?" he asked.

Wilma could only hope and pray she had to face that situation. "When she comes back, I'll tell her that I ransacked her room looking for clues. She'll understand. She'll know that we did it because we cared," she said.

"When she comes back, will you promise me that you'll go for counselling?" the officer asked.

It took all of Wilma's self-control not to lash out. How dare he say something so hurtful? "I promise you. If you find her and bring her back to me, I'll go and see six psychiatrists if that's what you want me to do," she said meekly.

"One will do," the officer replied.

As they left the Derksen home, the more vocal of the two officers couldn't help but deliver a parting shot.

"Look, who do you want to have egg on your face? You or me?" he asked.

"Me," replied Wilma.

. . . .

The doorbell rang. Heidi Harms was standing on the front steps, bag in hand packed with all kinds of goodies for her long-awaited weekend with Candace. The excitement was all over her face.

Cliff and Wilma were stunned. In all the confusion they had neglected to call Heidi's parents to explain the situation and cancel the visit. And here she now was. Her father, Dave, was sitting on the street in his car. Wilma waved for him to come inside.

"Heidi, I'm so sorry I didn't call. Candace isn't home," Wilma explained.

"Isn't home?" Heidi asked. "What do you mean?"

Wilma struggled to find the right words.

"We don't know what has happened to her. She didn't come home from school yesterday," she said.

Heidi's father had now joined them in the doorway.

"Candace didn't come home from school," Wilma repeated. "We don't know where she is."

"She knew I was coming," Heidi said.

"Heidi, I don't think she had a choice. She was looking forward to your coming so much. Nothing would have kept her from coming home. That's why we think something terrible must have happened to keep her from coming home from school," said Wilma. "But we're having a hard time convincing the police that she didn't run away. You know she wouldn't run away."

Heidi was now sobbing. "Candace wouldn't run away … I just know she wouldn't run away. We were going to have so much fun," she said.

Wilma explained to Heidi and her father exactly where things stood, promising to keep them updated on any developments. She watched helplessly as Heidi walked back to the car with her father, devastated at what she'd just heard.

....

Wilma barely had time to digest the heartbreaking development when the phone rang again. It was Mary Wiebe, the mother of Candace's school crush.

"Did Candace come home?" Mary asked. "David is so worried."

Wilma said they were still searching.

"Is your family with you?" Mary asked.

"No, Cliff's family lives in Saskatchewan and mine live in British Columbia. We really don't have anyone in the city," said Wilma.

"You shouldn't be alone now. You need your family," Mary replied.

"It's really okay," said Wilma. Truthfully, it really wasn't. There was nothing they needed more right now than family.

"Can I come over?" Mary asked.

Wilma said she was most certainly welcome. Mary promised to be right over.

....

The rest of the day was a blur of activity—phone calls from out-of-town family members, friends from church and more frustrating conversations with police.

One of the initial investigators called back just after lunch, saying they were convinced Candace had chosen to go missing based on some interviews they'd conducted with her friends. "We are convinced more than ever that she ran away and that you, her parents, are the problem," he repeated.

Cliff and Wilma were at a loss for words. They were relying on police to assist them, yet felt like they were wasting precious time arguing and trying to assign blame.

Mary Wiebe had come, as promised, and was proving to be an enormous help at this most difficult time. Despite never having previously met, she was extremely gracious and compassionate. The Derksens soon found themselves facing similar acts of grace.

Dave Loewen, Cliff's boss, was back on the phone explaining he'd made arrangements for a civilian search party to begin looking for Candace immediately. He had spoken with Dave DeFehr, a prominent Winnipeg busi- nessman whose family owned a successful local furniture store. DeFehr also served as president of the Camp Arnes board and was prepared to assist in any way he could. That included calling two Winnipeg lawyers for a briefing about the parameters and expectations of an organized private search.

Loewen had been busy, calling other Arnes board members, teachers from Mennonite Brethren and other community leaders. It was close to mid-afternoon when the masses began assembling, More than two dozen people, all on short notice, arrived at MBCI ready to lend a hand. They were met at the school by a different police officer who had been briefed by Loewen about what was happening.

The officer explained how they could search public areas without any difficulties but to be careful when approaching any private property. Police warned the group to ensure they obtained permission to search such a premise and have the property owner accompany them should they begin exploring any enclosures, such as a garage or shed.

The searches broke into smaller groups of two or three and were assigned a picture of Candace and a street map. Each group was given a different area to cover.

Cliff and Wilma were stunned at the kindness of so many people.

....

It was late afternoon when the searchers, many of them not properly dressed for the now bitterly cold temperatures, began arriving back at the school. There was little progress to report.

One of the groups had stumbled across two abandoned homes which they suggested police may want to follow up on. They believed the properties might make a good spot for someone to hide or be hidden.

Dave DeFehr and his wife, Ester, had also participated in the ground-level search and spoke of an unusual encounter with one family.

The couple said they were explaining the situation to an older man when his son, perhaps in his mid-twenties, showed an obvious reaction upon hearing Candace's name. He had appeared flustered, dropping some change he'd been carrying in his hand. When they tried to ask the younger man a few questions, the homeowner intervened and cut them off.

The DeFehrs reported this incident, and the address, to police.

Cliff and Wilma had provided snacks and hot beverages to many of the searches who'd stopped by their home that afternoon. They felt it was the least they could do.

They'd also spoken with Harold Jantz, a family friend who was editor of the *Mennonite Brethren Herald*, for advice about getting word about Candace out to some of the bigger local media outlets.

Each searcher was also asked to keep Candace in their prayers, especially when they attended church the following morning.

The final visitor on this long day was Pastor John Epp, along with his wife, Katie. It was exactly what the Derksens needed. There were words of wisdom, of comfort and Bible readings which helped put their faith into perspective at this most difficult time.

"I know you couldn't sleep last night. I also know that you are very tired and that you are going to need your sleep to keep up your strength in the days ahead," the pastor turned to Wilma and said before leaving. It was as if he'd been with her the entire time as she maintained her overnight vigil at the front window.

"You can sleep now. You can be at peace. There are others who will be praying for Candace tonight. Now there are others to help carry your load."

6

How does one prepare for a crisis? Usually we think of stockpiling money, food and basic supplies; but that wasn't what was needed in this crisis. As we faced the police and our loss, we needed something else. We needed support, wisdom, human resources and confidence. But how do you stockpile such things?

....

SUNDAY DECEMBER 2, 1984

It had been another excruciating night, filled with worry and regret. Wilma Derksen couldn't stop thinking about her final conversation with Candace, about rejecting her request for a ride home from school.

Cliff Derksen was struggling to stay strong for his weary wife while dealing primarily with police officers who didn't seem to be grasping the dire situation they were facing.

The couple was greeted on this morning with some promising news—two new plainclothes detectives had been assigned to the case. Cliff and Wilma hoped their fresh eyes would bring some much needed clarity to the case. Their hopes were dashed immediately when the officers showed up at their door shortly after 8 a.m.

"She's coming back tomorrow," one of them said. "Trust our experience. Kids her age stay with friends for the weekend and then come back Monday for school. It's happened over and over again. Besides, she's been sighted by two people."

Cliff and Wilma both felt their hearts skip a beat. Yet any excitement was quickly tempered by the almost cocky nature of the two cops.

"They're lying. They didn't see her," Wilma said.

"There is something in this case you aren't telling us. There is something missing here," one of the officers replied.

Cliff couldn't believe they were on this same, never-ending merry-go-round. He was about to say something when Wilma jumped in.

"Yes, it doesn't make sense, does it?" she said, attempting to defuse what was quickly becoming a very uncomfortable situation. "There is something missing. There is something wrong. It doesn't add up, and that's the dreadful part of it. We don't have that answer either. That piece you think is missing is the piece that is scaring the living daylights out of us."

Police continued to stay the same course, asking the same tiresome questions which had already been answered. Only there was a new twist. The officers included a story about a family in southern Manitoba which happened to be Mennonite—or maybe it was Hutterite, they weren't sure—who discovered their daughter missing. The couple then took advantage of the fact she'd run away to produce a bogus ransom note, hoping to cash in on the situation.

Cliff and Wilma just stood there with blank looks on their faces. Surely the officers couldn't be serious.

"We've been questioning all her friends. Some of them believe she could have run away. Did you know that you could be described as overbearing?" one of the officers asked.

Wilma felt as if they were being pushed into a corner, bullied and tormented while the police analyzed every aspect of their family at the expense of finding out what had really happened to Candace.

She sighed. "Yes, I know I can be overbearing," said Wilma. "But Candace has always prided herself that she can handle me."

The officers had no further questions—or lectures— but said they were going to keep an eye on the Derksens' church that morning in case Candace showed up.

Once they were gone, Cliff and Wilma couldn't help but share a small laugh.

"It's a pity they're going to spend all morning in their car, in the cold weather, watching a church for nothing," said Wilma.

"They should wait inside. They might learn something," Cliff said without missing a beat.

....

Harold Jantz had worked his magic, getting a small story and picture of Candace in the pages of the *Winnipeg Sun* that morning. The coverage led to a slew of other media calls throughout the day. Cliff and Wilma spoke with several different reporters, believing every little bit of publicity would help at this point.

There were several visitors throughout the day, including Candace's best friend Heidi Harms and her parents, Dave and Fran.

Dave Loewen had come up with several ideas, including speaking with Crime Stoppers about possibly offering a reward. Loewen suggested they strike a formal civilian search committee that could act as a liaison with police. He believed a more organized, intensive ground search could be done. Cliff volunteered to be a part of the committee.

Wilma's parents arrived that afternoon on a flight from British Columbia. They had made arrangements to come to Winnipeg for emotional support and to assist with Odia and Syras.

Later that night, Wilma explained how harsh the police had been during their dealings so far. They discussed their Mennonite faith and how investigators seemed to be drawing unfair stereotypes from it.

Wilma continued to pore through Candace's room, hoping to find any type of hint as to where her daughter might be. She scanned a shelf where several cassette tapes sat. One of them was of special significance. Wilma recalled the day Candace had burst into the kitchen as she made cookies, a smile on her face.

"Mom, I found my song, and I want you to hear it," Candace had said.

"Is it rock?" Wilma asked.

"No, you'll like it. It's by Michael W. Smith. It's a song that's just mine. I like the words and the music," Candace replied.

"What's it about?" Wilma asked.

"Friends," said Candace.

Wilma had joined her daughter that day, sitting in her bedroom listening to the song. It was beautiful.

Now, a few years later, Wilma was playing the tape for her own mother.

> Packing up the dreams God planted
> In the fertile soil of you.
> Can't believe the hopes He's granted
> Means a chapter in your life is through.
> But we'll keep you close as always
> It won't even seem you're gone.
> 'Cause our hearts in big and small ways
> Will keep the love that keeps us strong.
> And friends are friends forever
> If the Lord's the Lord of them.
> And a friend will not say "never"
> 'Cause the welcome will not end.
> Though it's hard to let you know
> In the Father's hands we know.
> That a lifetime's not too long to live as friends.

....

MONDAY DECEMBER 3, 1984

School was back in session—and Candace Derksen was nowhere to be found. Cliff and Wilma took no solace in the fact police had been proven wrong. They only hoped now the seriousness of the situation would truly be realized.

Sleep continued to be elusive, but life didn't stop moving. And the start of a new week, filled will all its routines, seemed almost too difficult to face with their daughter still missing.

The family was buoyed by an increasing groundswell of support. Dave Loewen had organized the first meeting of the civilian search committee for later that day. Cliff planned to attend, and Wilma felt like she needed to be there as well. Cliff's only concern was the emotional toll it might take.

"I promise I won't cry or make a scene. I won't act like a mother. I'll be part of the working team," she told her husband. "I'll be totally professional."

"That's not what I want. You can be a mother. You don't have to put yourself through this," said Cliff.

Wilma insisted this was something she had to do.

. . . .

They sat around a table in a private meeting room, sleeves rolled up and ready to work. Dave Loewen had done amazing work arranging this meeting in such a short period of time.

Others in the room included Dave Teigrob, the vice-principal of MBCI; Henry Wadel, a teacher at the school; Harold Jantz, the editor of the *Mennonite Brethren Herald*; and Dave and Ester DeFehr. Cliff and Wilma were overwhelmed by the support. This was the community coming together in the most incredible way.

Ester DeFehr was the first to speak. She had been in conversation with Winnipeg police and had discovered an organization called Child Find which she thought could provide some assistance. She promised to look into the issue further and report back at a future meeting.

Jantz began discussing the need to heighten awareness of Candace's case through increased media exposure. He suggested Cliff and Wilma might want to go on television to make a statement. "The media won't be hostile. They're sympathetic and want to help," he explained.

Wilma was having difficulty with the idea, wondering how she could possibly compose herself long enough to stand in front of strangers and make a plea for her daughter to come home. She promised to think about it.

Wilma was struggling to keep her tears from flowing and excused herself from the meeting. She felt like she needed to get back to the telephone. "I've been away too long," she explained. She encouraged her husband to stay. He would get a ride from the school and meet her back at home.

Once she reached the car, Wilma's emotions got the best of her. She felt as if she was losing control. She was running on fumes and didn't know how much more she could take.

....

"We think you should do it."

Wilma was stunned that her parents actually thought a televised plea was a good idea. She had arrived home moments earlier, met immediately with the disappointment of learning there had been no updates on Candace.

Talk quickly turned to the meeting, where Wilma explained what had happened during the meeting and how she didn't think she could handle a public appearance. But all the signs seemed to be pushing her in that direction. That afternoon, two of her former instructors from Red River Community College showed up at her door offering support.

The instructors, who had taught her journalism and public relations, also agreed with the committee's recommendation. "The public is out there. You need to solicit their help," they said.

Cliff arrived home from the meeting, stressing the importance and urgency of such a plea.

"Wilma, we have to go on television. We have to do this for Candace," he said.

"Will you be here with me?" Wilma asked.

"Yes, I'll be here," he replied.

Cliff walked back to the front door, stepped outside and waved his hands. Two local television news station trucks were parked on the street, just waiting for their cue. They had been contacted by the committee earlier in the day.

Wilma dashed upstairs to freshen up, returning moments later to find her living room now resembling a television studio. She sat down on the couch, taking deep breaths. Her two instructors were still in the home, staying behind for moral support.

"For Candace," one of them mouthed as the cameras started to roll.

....

Several police officers stopped by later that evening with an unusual request. They wanted one of Candace's shoes.

Wilma was afraid to ask why they wanted it. She believed they might use it to try and trace Candace's scent with one of their trained police dogs. But with the fresh snow which had fallen since last Friday, she wondered how much of a track they could actually get at this point.

Police also spoke of an aerial search they'd conducted that afternoon of the general area. Although it hadn't turned up anything suspicious, Cliff and Wilma were happy with the effort.

Slowly, but surely, it appeared police were finally starting to realize what was happening. The Derksens believed the formation of the civilian search committee, along with newspaper, television and radio interviews they'd now done, were putting increasing pressure on law enforcement. And that was a good thing.

Police also had one other intriguing bit of news. They had discovered there was a slightly older teenage girl living in the neighbourhood who actually had a striking resemblance to Candace. But this particular girl had a long list of issues, including a drug addiction, and had several unsavoury associates.

Police didn't say it, but Cliff and Wilma couldn't help but wonder if Candace may have been mistaken for this troubled teen and grabbed by someone looking to settle a score.

It seemed farfetched. But at this point they weren't going to rule anything out.

....

They watched the evening newscasts with great interest, relieved that Candace's story was being told to an even wider audience. Wilma was happy she'd been talked into doing it, especially after seeing Candace's picture splashed across the television.

In a late-night conversation with her parents, Wilma learned why they'd been so insistent on her doing a public plea. Her parents explained how their community in British Columbia had been impacted by the case of Clifford Olson, a serial killer who would ultimately kill 11 children in the Fraser Valley. Wilma shuddered at the thought her daughter could have fallen victim to a similar monster.

It was now well past midnight when Wilma, unable to sleep yet again, climbed out of bed and made her way back to the kitchen table.

Alone with her thoughts, Wilma's mind was racing at an incredible speed.

She suddenly recalled an earlier chance encounter with the people who shared the other side of their duplex. Wilma had learned the main occupant was an aspiring local wrestler, which explained why she often heard banging through their walls.

On the very night Candace had gone missing, Wilma had run into a young man outside the home who she'd never seen before. He explained he was also a wrestler, visiting Winnipeg for an upcoming match and staying with his friend.

Wilma could feel her heart beginning to race once again.

What if Candace had been grabbed right outside her own home, by this testosterone-fuelled muscleman? What if Candace was being held right next door?

Wilma had to talk herself out of racing outside and pounding on their door, right now, demanding to see her missing daughter. As the minutes passed, she realized how silly her theory was.

Still, it was going to be another sleepless night.

7

Clifford and Wilma Derksen say they are convinced their daughter Candace, 13, has been abducted but they say they haven't given up hope she will come home.

"It's a terrible feeling," Wilma Derksen said during an interview in the living room of their Herbert Avenue home. "There is just nothing concrete. Not one clue in any direction."

The Derksens say Candace's disappearance has taken its toll on them and their two other children, Odia, 9, and Syras, 3.

They say they have been in a kind of suspended animation since Candace went missing, jumping every time the telephone rings and expecting to see their daughter's smiling face every time they answer the door.

The police telephone the Derksens every morning to inform them on the progress of their search.

"We are wishing we could believe it was a runaway," Clifford said. "That would be a relief ... that she was OK and with a friend or something. But my mind doesn't rest with that thought."

While the disappearance has been hard on them, the Derksens say they've been able to cope, partly because of the support they've received from hundreds of people in their community and because of their faith.

"I don't think we could make it without faith," Candace's father said. "With two children, we can't be down all the time. I had to realize four days after she disappeared that you can't put a three-year-old on hold."

The Derksens say they find themselves wondering whether she is still alive.

"We seem to be mourning her ... we are mourning her departure, then we catch ourselves and say she might come back. We go from hope to despair ... and fear," Wilma said.

"We don't know where she is," Clifford said. "We don't know if she is coming back."

The couple says certain times during the day, particularly the late evening and early morning when they are alone, are more difficult than others.

Clifford said the mornings are very difficult.

"I'd wake her up in the mornings and get her out of bed," he said. "I'd pull her out of bed and we'd have our little play-fights. She loved that and I enjoyed that. I miss that."

Wilma said she had become accustomed to having Candace walk in the door after school, ready to share the day's experiences.

The children have also missed their big sister.

Candace's parents describe her as a typical teenager with the usual problems. She loved her friends, loved sports and wasn't always crazy about school.

She had encountered academic problems in school earlier this year and her first report card's marks weren't as high as her parents would have liked.

However, they said they feel she had been improving just prior to her disappearance and her grades reflected that.

As well, the Derksens note police interviews with friends didn't turn up any plans for running away.

Friday and Saturday nights also are difficult, because those were family nights. Friday the family stayed home together and Saturday they went swimming, one of Candace's favourite sports, along with horseback riding and volleyball.

There are other times when break in the routine or a memory of Candace makes it difficult to carry on, they said.

"Just setting the supper table," Wilma said.

Also, she said, there is the lack of music coming from Candace's bedroom. Candace used to listen to a tape she made of contemporary Christian music which included a song entitled "Friends are Friends Forever."

The song suggests people can be friends with each other even if they are physically separated.

"She had that tape by her bed and clicked on it every night," Clifford recalled. "Now that she is not here, those words mean a lot to us because she is separated from us."

—*WINNIPEG FREE PRESS*

....

TUESDAY DECEMBER 5, 1984

The publicity was working. It seemed as if every Winnipegger was now getting to know the name Candace Derksen.

Yet there was also a dark side to the information campaign. Police had warned the search committee there would likely be a deluge of calls who—either driven by personal agendas or perhaps mental illness—would be looking to make themselves a part of the story.

Sure enough, the calls began trickling in.

A couple in the Elmwood area called several media outlets, claiming they'd seen a young girl being dragged away by two young men on Friday afternoon. They claimed to have phoned police, only to be swatted away by a rude officer who told them "Candace is just another runaway" and couldn't possibly be linked to what they saw.

However, holes began to form in their story—including the fact they later changed their timeline to suggest it was actually prior to 4 p.m. when they witnessed the incident. As well, they conceded it was possible these were just kids playing around.

Several strangers began calling the Derksens to speak of their own horror stories. Some just wanted to vent about police, some had theories about what may have happened to Candace, while others seemed to be decent people wishing to express their concern.

Police were also softening their stance, at least in public, by admitting their concern was growing by the day.

Insp. Bill Heintz of the juvenile division told the media that the runaway teen theory was beginning to look less likely. "Statistics show kids who run away usually return within two days. While there's no evidence suggesting foul play, we're certainly concerned about the situation," he said.

There were a total of 76 missing youths in Winnipeg on the day Candace vanished—47 girls, 29 boys. In total, police had investigated 4,455 missing children cases in the previous year alone. Heintz later told a reporter they were getting calls from many other parents concerned about the volume of publicity in the Candace Derksen case. "To a certain extent, we're hearing from them asking for similar attention," he said.

The search committee had started blanketing parts of the city with bright orange posters bearing the words "Have You Seen Candace?" The highly visible signs included a description of Candace and her most recent school picture.

Several civilian searches were also underway. Nearly 500 students from MBCI spent part of their afternoon retracing the route Candace normally walked. They also scoped out the riverbank and railway tracks in the area. The students blitzed the area with posters, getting many local businesses to hang them in their windows.

It was believed to be the largest civilian search ever done in Winnipeg's history.

Cliff and Wilma continued to do media interviews, including a live radio hit with popular radio show host Peter Warren. His daily morning show on top-rated CJOB would be heard around the province.

"Mrs. Derksen, I have an audience of thousands who listen every day. What if Candace is listening right now? What would you like to say?" Warren asked.

Wilma was caught off-guard. How does one answer such a question?

"Oh, Candace, come home. We're waiting for you," she said. In reality, Wilma doubted her daughter would ever hear those words.

. . . .

The committee had vowed to meet every day, even if just for a short time, until the mystery had been solved. Wilma had stayed away this time, not wanting to have another emotional breakdown. But Cliff was present, along with the same committee members who had gathered during their initial meeting.

Ester DeFehr had been conducting extensive research on the Child Find organization, learning they had chapters in Calgary, Vancouver, Oakville and London Ontario. She had also spoken with someone from the Missing Children's Society, based out of Edmonton.

All of the agencies were eager to lend their advice and assistance with Candace's case. DeFehr was going to send them a photo and description of Candace which would promptly be distributed through their extensive contacts across the country. DeFehr had also been on the phone with representatives from the National Centre for Missing and Exploited Children in Washington. The non-profit organization was ready to help as well.

One of the main items during this meeting was discussing the creation of the Candace Derksen Search Fund, which would be handled by Camp Arnes. The committee would go public with a call for donations, which would help pay for costs associated with the ongoing search.

There was also early discussion about a reward fund. Committee members decided to speak with police about this issue, not wanting to go above their heads and do anything which might jeopardize the ongoing investigation.

Other issues raised including the possibility of hiring a private detective, which Child Find had told DeFehr was always a good idea in these types of cases.

The meeting ended with one final decision—a prayer chain would be created immediately. Everyone on the committee agreed this was an important step in the process. Volunteers would be recruited through Camp Arnes to get the ball rolling.

Wilma was thrilled by this development. It was a simple yet poignant gesture—a list of names is created of people who wish to support each other in a time of need. To get involved, you simply phone the next person on the list, pass on a prayer request, pray together, then hang up.

....

I'm calling on behalf of the Candace Derksen search committee. We appreciate all prayer on behalf of Candace, her family and the search. The Derksens say a sincere 'Thank You.' The police have worked hard all week. Students from Candace's school have searched and distributed posters. The citizens' search committee meets daily to plan the search in co-opera-tion with the police. Clues and suggestions of friends and citizens have been followed up.

There are no leads to date.

The search has now gone national through Child Find, the news, friends and Christian camps. Please continue to pray for information of Candace's where-abouts, Candace's safety and return, the Derksens, and wisdom for the citizens' search committee.

Prayer is our only hope.

....

The days were becoming a blur, painfully long for the Derksens yet seemingly moving far too quickly.

Sleep continued to be the enemy, especially for Wilma who was continuing to maintain a nightly vigil at her front window.

Police had given their blessing to offer a reward but had some advice about the wording of such a plea. Investigators told the committee to say things like "for the safe return of Candace" and for information which "gives" her whereabouts, not just "leads" to it.

A major press conference would soon be held to announce the reward. Cliff and Wilma had agreed to appear to repeat their public plea.

Another 2,000 "Missing" posters had been ordered for distribution around Winnipeg.

Tips were continuing to pour in, many of them extremely sketchy in nature. Wilma had started receiving phone calls from psychics, something police warned her was likely to happen. The first had been a man from Kenora, Ontario, about two hours east of Winnipeg. He wanted to know if Wilma would send him a strand of Candace's hair. The man claimed he had a fool-proof system for giving them a location on Candace "within 3,000 miles."

"Three thousand miles? That isn't exactly what one would call terribly accurate," she said to her husband.

"At least we'd know if she's still in the province," Cliff said.

They agreed to politely decline the offer.

Many of the calls brought a much-needed sense of comic relief. The Derksens even began giving nicknames to some of the callers—"pendulum lady", "the white house ghost", "the culvert man", "the dreamer", "the old voice."

Another young man showed up at Camp Arnes, claiming he was a "born again believer" who had psychic powers. He claimed to have seen Candace in a "dark place, probably outside the city limits."

The Derksens learned police were being flooded with similar tips, including some tarot card readers who claimed Candace was most certainly with someone she knew.

In a 24-hour period alone, the Derksens received a total of 75 calls, mostly from strangers. There were at least nine reported sightings of Candace. All were passed on to police, none were found to be credible.

It was all becoming a bit too much to handle.

....

With hope for a happy ending seemingly gone, Cliff and Wilma found themselves spending an increasing amount of time focusing not just on what had happened—but on why it had happened.

Stories and rumours had started circulating through the community, with some speculating that Candace may have been targeted for a sexual purpose. It was difficult to fathom for the Derksens; the thought their sweet and innocent child could be the victim of something so deviant.

Dave Loewen had actually raised the issue at one of their recent search committee meetings, in which Cliff and Wilma were both absent. Loewen said he'd been speaking with a concerned citizen who suggested they investigate the possibility Candace was abducted for the purpose of bringing her into some kind of child sex ring being run by pedophiles. Although there was no proof to suggest this was the case, the woman seemed convinced.

"She suggested high-priced men pay big dollars for this kind of deviation," Loewen told the committee during the meeting. "She thinks we should seriously consider checking hotels where girls like Candace might be forced to work." The committee recommended they speak directly with the police morals and child abuse units to raise the possibility.

Ester DeFehr said she'd spoken with people from the Pregnancy Distress organization where she worked about Candace's case. The director, Ellen Jones, told DeFehr she felt strongly Candace might indeed be a victim "of some kind of sex ring."

DeFehr visited the Derksens later that day, filling them in on the discussion they'd had.

"Was Candace experienced?" DeFehr asked, clearly uncomfortable at even having to raise the issue.

"Ester, I don't think Candace was. I think she was much more innocent that people knew. I can't be certain, of course," Wilma said after a few moments of thinking about her question.

"It really doesn't matter. Even for someone who is sexually active, rape is violent. I've talked to girls at Pregnancy Distress who've been raped. They've all said that while it's happening, the body goes into some kind of shock. It's like they leave their bodies to hide," said DeFehr.

"You mean she wouldn't have felt..." Wilma began.

"No, she would have been so scared. She really wouldn't have understood," said DeFehr.

"I wanted her first experience to be wonderful. I wanted her to be with someone who would love her," Wilma said, softly.

"The emotions go numb, Wilma. It would have been dreadful, but it doesn't mean that she can't have a good marriage still, if ... Girls do get over rape. With counselling, with help," DeFehr said.

....

A good two-way line of communication had been established between the civilian search committee and Winnipeg police. Both sides were constantly updating and sharing information. Police had now assigned four

officers to work the case full-time, a sure sign they no longer believed this was a routine runaway case.

"Everything possible is being done," said Insp. Bill
Heintz.

Dave DeFehr shared an interesting conversation he'd
had with a young man who believed he saw Candace
hanging around at a local curling rink with four other
young girls on December 1st.

The man—who lived in the neighbourhood and had
seen Candace many times before—was positive it was her.
He didn't know who the other girls were.

The committee also spoke with three local private
detectives who were reluctant to get involved at this
stage. They believed the investigation was best left to
police for now, but remained open to assisting down
the road.

There was continued good news on the media front,
as *Canada A.M.* had agreed to do a national story on
Candace's case. The *Toronto Sun* was also picking up
the trail.

Donations were rolling in, and the committee was
getting ready to make a public announcement about a
$2,000 reward in conjunction with police.

Police had followed up on the earlier tip from searchers about a neighbourhood home where a young man
had acted suspiciously. It turned out the family was actually harbouring a 16-year-old runaway, which explained
their odd behaviour. There was absolutely no connection
to Candace.

Cliff and Wilma had also penned a personal note which was being distributed to 76 churches in Winnipeg for inclusion in an upcoming bulletin.

Finally, the committee decided that the couple should make one final public appeal just before Christmas.

....

It was now nearly two full weeks since Candace had vanished. The trail was growing cold. Wilma Derksen was lost in thought, in her kitchen, when the telephone rang. It was such a frequent event that the sound barely even registered anymore. She instinctively picked up the receiver.

"Hello," said Wilma.

There was silence on the other end of the line.

"Hello," Wilma repeated.

She could someone breathing.

Finally, a voice began to whisper.

"Mom.... Mom."

Wilma immediately recognized this for what it was and slammed the receiver down.

It was yet another crank call.

8

Her name was Theresa. And she had an incredible tale to tell.

The grade seven student at John Henderson Junior High had contacted Harold Jantz, the editor of the *Mennonite Brethren Herald*, with information about Candace Derksen.

"I saw her standing outside the Zellers store on Henderson Highway," Theresa said.

"When was this?" asked Jantz.

"December 11th."

Theresa continued with her story as Jantz scribbled down notes.

"I walked up to her and said 'What are you doing here?' She asked me to do her a favour," said Theresa. "I kept asking her what she was doing here, why she wasn't home. She told me to make up a big lie, to say she was kidnapped. To say to her parents that she was okay, that she was still alive."

Theresa said she'd been scared to come forward.

"She said if I told the truth I'd get my head kicked in. She told me 'I know something about you'."

Theresa claimed Candace was with an older boy, perhaps in his late teens. She believed his name was Randy and gave a full description to Jantz—blue eyes, long hair past his shoulders, an earring and a faint moustache. She claimed he stood there beside Candace the whole time, never saying a word. There was another girl as well, maybe 15 years old, standing near a dark van the man appeared to own.

"Candace said she would get in touch with me again, but she hasn't," said Theresa.

She knew Candace through a mutual friend and claimed she was positive this was her.

Jantz had taken detailed notes and thanked Theresa for her time. She claimed to have already shared much of this story with police—a detail Jantz found somewhat alarming. As a good friend of the Derksens, this was not just another news story to him. It was personal.

A quick call to police dashed any hopes Jantz had of a major development. Investigators were well aware of Theresa. They had interviewed her at least half a dozen times. Her story seemed to change with each passing day. Police were confident she was simply a troubled girl looking for attention. She had no credibility. She had no information about Candace.

Jantz was devastated.

. . . .

The signs of the season were all around them. But Cliff and Wilma Derksen didn't feel much like celebrating Christmas this year.

Wilma had completed much of her shopping in November, before Candace vanished. Yet just days from the holiday, those gifts remained unwrapped in her home.

Local media were asking plenty of expected questions about what Christmas was going to be like without their oldest daughter. It was impossible to answer, other than to say it would be like every other day during the past three weeks—sad, empty and certainly incomplete.

Police had continued to stay in touch with the Derksens but were reporting little, if any, progress. Officers would periodically stop by the family home, bringing items of clothing they had recovered from various parts of the city to check if they were Candace's.

None of the items had been a match.

Jantz had told them about his interview with the girl who claimed to have seen Candace outside Zellers. Cliff and Wilma knew it was bogus the second he mentioned the girl claiming Candace threatened to "kick her head in." That wasn't their daughter. She would never say something like that.

And yet, there were times when doubt began to seep in, whether the family questioned how much they really knew Candace. Does any parent really know their child inside and out?

There were more rumours, more troubling phone calls. Yet the daily volume seemed to be going down.

Somehow, word began spreading that Candace's body had been found floating at the floodway on the outskirts of Winnipeg. It was false, of course. But certainly painful to hear.

The search committee had expressed some frustration to police, questioning why investigators couldn't conduct searches of private property. Police explained they couldn't just invade someone's home, kicking down doors and looking in closets. They needed evidence and cold hard proof in order to first obtain a warrant.

"It's no longer realistic to think she would have voluntarily disappeared. There had to be others involved, and I find it hard to understand why no information has come forward," Dave Loewen, the co-ordinator of the search committee, told reporters.

Politicians—municipal, provincial and federal—were also getting involved. Bill Blaikie, a Manitoba member of parliament, sent a letter to federal justice minister John Crosbie saying this case showed the need to get tougher on crimes involving children.

"Her disappearance has provided members of our community with a tragic opportunity to become acquainted with the facts concerning the numbers of missing children and the not unreasonable fear that many such children have been abducted for purposes of child pornography," Blaikie wrote.

The rumour mill had apparently spun all the way to Ottawa.

....

It was one of the strangest encounters they'd ever had. A middle-aged man, dressed in grubby clothing and appearing to be in dire need of a shower, appeared at the Derksens door around 10 p.m. one evening in mid-December.

He had some information—not about Candace directly, but about the way they were going about trying to find her.

"You don't know anything. You lead a sheltered life. How do you know what a criminal thinks? What do you know about street life?" the man began.

He appeared to be well versed in all of those categories.

"Look at you. You're Mennonites. Have you ever been to a prison?" he asked.

Cliff and Wilma said they hadn't, not even to visit.

"You don't know anything. I've served nine years," he said. "Maybe I have something you need. I know how a criminal thinks."

The Derksens were intrigued. Perhaps he was on to something here. They invited their rather unusual guest to continue, offering him a cup of coffee in the process.

The man was blunt about his history. He claimed he was now on a better path following his release, including finding full-time work. He wanted Cliff to come for a ride. "I'll show you what kind of neighbourhood you live in," he said.

Cliff's parents had arrived days earlier from Saskatoon. His father agreed to go with them. Wilma and her mother exchanged worried glances.

"Maybe Candace isn't in this neighbourhood. Why do you want to concentrate on this neighbourhood? Personally, I think she was probably picked up by a car. She could be out of the city by now," Wilma said.

"That's where you're wrong. They don't do things like that. They stay where they are, they don't travel around much," the man insisted.

Cliff agreed it might be a good idea and climbed inside the stranger's black van, his father joining him.

Wilma couldn't believe this was really happening.

....

They returned to the home late at night, safe and sound and armed with a new appreciation for life on the "dark side."

"The black van wasn't the worst. I nearly didn't go with him when I saw the old freezer in the back," Cliff said, laughing. "He told us it was in there for traction in the winter."

Cliff and his father had gone on a fascinating tour of the area. Their host had pointed out the homes of every known drug dealer and biker. He'd also singled out several sheds, trailers and garages he suggested would make perfect hiding places for a criminal. They made notes of all the locations and would share them with the civilian search committee and police.

....

One of Candace's friends, Kiersten Loewen, had written a touching poem which captured the feelings of so many in the community. She got it published in the *Winnipeg Free Press* just days before Christmas.

"I knew her,"
I claim
But did I really?
Candace, always smiling, laughing,

Giving of herself,
To strangers and friends alike.
Candace, the one who didn't seem to need anything.
No one thought that anything would happen to her.
"Not to Candace,"
They say.
"She's so sweet, kind and giving.
Not to her."
Well they were wrong.
Something did happen to her.
And now I fear she might be dead.
No more to see the sun again,
The rain again,
Feel pain again,
No more to cheer me up again,
Praise God again.
Candace
Where are you?

....

THURSDAY DECEMBER 20, 1984

Wilma didn't know how she was going to make it through her statement.

The Derksens were preparing to face the cameras to make one more public appeal for information. With the holidays just around the corner, there was a fear tips and leads were going to dry up as people were preoccupied with their personal lives.

They arrived at Mennonite Brethren Collegiate, prepared for an emotional scene. Wilma had practised reading her statement out loud at home but couldn't get through it without crying.

Insp. Roman Giereck of the juvenile division told media how they'd already followed up close to 200 calls from the public without any success.

"This is very strange that we haven't been able to come up with anything," he said.

The microphone was turned over to Wilma to make her plea. Cliff stood stoically at her side.

"Candace," she began, facing a throng of reporters and cameras. "If you are watching, we want you to know how much we love you. And no matter what happened, nothing will change our love. We just want you to come home. We want to be a family again. Odia and Syras talk about you all the time, and even Percy the cat misses you.

"If someone is keeping you from coming home, I'd like to plead with that person to let you go. We're not seeking revenge or even justice. All we want is for Candace to come home."

Wilma had managed to keep the tears at bay. For now, anyway.

"The worst is not knowing. As long as we don't know what happened to Candace, we are going to worry. Is she cold? Does she have enough to eat? Is she hurt? That is why we're appealing to everyone," Wilma continued reading.

"And for those of you who have backed us and cooked for us, prayed for us and informed us of what you have seen or what you know, we can't thank you enough.

Your concern and love has offset the horror that we are feeling. It would be easier to accept whatever might have happened than to live with this torture of not knowing.

"More than anything in the world, we want Candace home for Christmas."

....

The press conference continued with a few questions from reporters. Many were focused on the family's plans for the holidays.

"We're still not sure what we're going to do," Wilma admitted. "We're hoping something breaks before then. But we're going to try to have a happy Christmas for our other two children."

She explained it had been exceptionally difficult to give Odia and Syras the attention they needed, and deserved.

"Sometimes I get to thinking about Candace so much I almost want to make a shrine of her things, and then I remember I have two other children who need love, too."

Cliff spoke as well, thanking police and the community for their efforts.

"We have been so surprised by the support, it has just been wonderful. We were very pleased with how quickly the police have responded. I guess I'm the emotional father, so once in a while I blow up at the police. But we're really grateful to them," he said.

"If they had a clue and they weren't doing anything about it, then we would be frustrated. But we have no clues and know they have no clues," added Wilma.

Dave Loewen also spoke about the work of the civilian search committee and the tremendous public response they'd received. He said it points to the need to create a specialized, full-time agency in the city such as Child Find.

"We feel quite strongly that the reason there has been so much compassion surrounding this case is that generally people hurt very much over the disappearance of children," said Loewen.

"There are many other parents in the city who have missing children. What the community is feeling now toward Candace they also feel in general."

He vowed the committee would continue meeting and brainstorming until they had a resolution.

Near the end of the event, Cliff had an accidental slip of the tongue when discussing Candace. He spoke of his daughter in the past tense.

"Candace had a short life, but if something positive can come of that, then we will be thankful."

....

Suzanne Shostal could only imagine what the Derksen family was going through. She went through her own traumatic experience less than a year earlier after her two-year-old twins vanished from her Saskatoon home.

Fortunately, a neighbour found them wandering the street 45 minutes later. During a moment of distraction, the kids had left the home thinking they could go play with a friend down the street.

The near-tragedy prompted Shostal to start a Child Find chapter in her hometown. And now she had come to Winnipeg to help those searching for Candace. She met face-to-face with the Derksens, assuring them the Saskatchewan chapter was doing everything they could to help.

"I know the terror I felt," said Shostal.

Shostal also spoke with members of the civilian search committee, who had expressed an interest in setting up a Winnipeg chapter down the road.

....

They certainly weren't in the holiday spirit—but that didn't stop those around the Derksen family from trying to make Christmas a special event.

Cliff and Wilma continued to be overwhelmed with the support shown by all those rallying around them. Although both sets of their parents had returned home, there was no shortage of love being sent their way.

They attended the Camp Arnes Christmas party, which Odia and Syras particularly enjoyed. Cliff and Wilma kept a low profile, not wanting to make anyone at the gathering feel like they couldn't properly enjoy it.

Still, it was difficult to take in. Seeing other families together, smiles on their faces, was a stark reminder that their family unit had been ripped apart.

Many people showed up at the Derksens bearing gifts on Christmas Eve. They included baking, decorations and toys for the children.

One young boy, who had played with Candace at camp in previous years, showed up with his mother to drop off a small Christmas tree he'd cut just for them.

There were also numerous Christmas Day dinner invitations. Yet the Derksens politely declined all of them, electing to spend December 25th home alone. They tried to stick to as many traditions as possible, which included attending church on Christmas Eve. Candace was included in everyone's prayers.

They returned home and watched as Odia and Syras opened their gifts. Later, Wilma broke down in her husband's arms, saying how difficult it had been to do that without Candace.

"Tradition is just too painful. The only way to deal with this is to do something that doesn't feel like Christmas," she said.

So they had stayed away from church on Christmas morning. The children played with their gifts, while Cliff and Wilma spent much of the day reading.

For dinner, they got in their car and headed out. There would be no home-cooked meal with all the trimmings.

They began driving, unsure of exactly where they would go. The kids wanted McDonald's, which Cliff and Wilma somewhat reluctantly agreed to.

It was closed.

They continued searching, eventually heading downtown and then west on Portage Avenue. It seemed as if the entire city had shut down.

"This is probably the most authentic Christmas we will ever have," Cliff said with a chuckle. "We're just like Joseph and Mary looking for a place to settle and finding nothing open."

The family finally found a small cafe where they grabbed a quick and greasy bite.

The food was terrible.

After dinner, they headed to the movies. They all agreed on *Pinocchio*.

It turned out to be a poor choice.

The family watched with sadness as an emotionally distraught Gepetto began walking the streets, looking for his lost, abducted son. Of course, the film would end on a happy note with a joyful reunion.

If only Walt Disney could have written the Candace Derksen story.

9

It had become a fairly common event—police officers calling or showing up at their front door. Yet every conversation still brought a sense of anticipation and dread.

Had they located a clue? Had one of their tips panned out?

Had Candace been found?

It was just a few days into the New Year when one of the main investigators called with a request. Police were hoping to get a copy of Candace's dental records.

"Not that we'll need them," the officer quickly added, perhaps realizing the ominous nature of the conversation.

"Actually, I don't know why we need them right now. It's just nice to have on hand," he said.

Police didn't have to say anything more. The Derksens understood.

....

The civilian search committee continued to meet on an almost daily basis. They had received more than $5,000 in public donations so far, most of which was earmarked for the reward that had yet to be claimed.

The group had taken a few days off during Christmas—but only because Cliff had insisted.

"Let things rest," he said convincingly.

Police had conducted another intensive search of the area on December 30th without any new developments.

It had been their most thorough one to date. Police had actually stopped dozens of cars travelling down Talbot Avenue, trying to find people who normally travelled the route on Friday afternoons to determine whether they might have seen anything a month earlier. Many of the officers who participated were volunteering their time.

The committee decided they would send a "heartfelt thanks via letter" to everyone involved in the operation.

Committee members were tossing around several ideas to keep Candace's story alive. One of the more unique ones was to approach local diary producers about putting Candace's face on the side of milk cartons. Dave Loewen had discovered this had never been in done in Canada before. He reported strong interest from police and promised to follow up.

There was also increasing discussion about hiring a private investigator. Many on the committee felt strongly that a fresh set of eyes might be a good step.

"This could be a whole new dimension," explained Loewen. He had been speaking with a private eye from Lincoln, Nebraska who specialized in missing person cases.

Police were lukewarm to the idea and told Loewen they wouldn't be able to share specific details of their investigation.

Still, Loewen and others thought it might be worth a shot. The main obstacle was cost. The self-employed sleuth would charge $375 for an initial consultation, plus airfare to fly to Winnipeg for a face-to-face meeting. From there, costs could go as high as $100,000 depending on the length and complexity of the work involved. The committee decided further debate on this issue would be needed at future meetings.

They had also sent a request to various Winnipeg churches, encouraging them to adopt Sunday, January 6th as a day of prayer—not just for Candace, but for all missing children in the province.

"According to the Winnipeg police, this is one of the most intense searches for missing persons in our city and the search is still very active," they wrote in the letter. "Christmas has come and gone for Cliff and Wilma Derksen and their two remaining children. It was painful. Peace yes, but no joy."

The committee included various statistics they'd obtained from police, including the fact that there were between 70–90 children missing in Winnipeg at any time.

"We simply cannot imagine the combined anguish of all those parents. We are convinced that we, as the body of Christ, have a ministry to such families," they wrote.

"The Christian community is a powerful resource. Friends and strangers alike from Ottawa to Victoria and particularly Winnipeg have, and continue to pray, to assist in the search and to share the pain. God alone can overrule evil. He knows the whereabouts of Candace and her welfare. But there is a struggle against the spiritual forces of evil."

....

It had been a quiet start to 1985 in the Derksen residence. Several out-of-town family members had visited after Christmas but had since returned home. The holidays were over. It was back to routine.

And that meant continuing to adjust to life without Candace.

The calls had slowed considerably. Candace's story still remained big news but it was clear many people were moving on with their lives. Cliff and Wilma weren't sure how they could do that without knowing what had happened to their daughter.

Wilma increasingly found herself lost in deep thought, staring blankly out the front window. There were other times she'd catch herself focusing her gaze on a stranger, consumed by thoughts that had been repeatedly put into her head by police investigators and other victims of child abductions.

"You will probably know Candace's abductor. It's probably someone from your community," they would say.

It was difficult to digest, but hard to ignore. Could someone in their circle of friends and acquaintances be responsible for the suffering they were going through?

They got an emotional boost in early January when the parents of another high-profile missing Canadian child called them.

Christine Jessop had been abducted near her home in Queensland, Ontario the previous October. The body of the nine-year-old girl had been found on New Year's Eve in another town about 50 kilometres away. An autopsy had revealed Christine had been raped and strangled. No arrests had been made in a case which had stunned the region.

Robert and Janet Jessop had heard about Candace's case in the midst of their own anguish. Now they were reach out to Cliff and Wilma.

"We hoped for the best and expected the worst," Robert said.

He explained how police had looked at him with a suspicious eye, asking him to take a polygraph test.

"That must have been so difficult," said Wilma.

"Yes. I took the test, though, because it's the only thing the police understand. I'm just glad I passed. The polygraph can be unreliable," he said.

Wilma couldn't help but wonder if Cliff might face the same scrutiny. The thought horrified her.

The Jessops had experienced many of the same things as the Derksens—crank calls, psychics offering their services and incredible support from their family, friends and community. And as difficult as it had been, the Jessops said there was a sense of relief in finally knowing what had happened to their daughter.

They told Cliff and Wilma they'd be praying for similar closure for them.

....

It was so difficult to gauge what impact the search for Candace was having on her two younger siblings. At the age of nine, Odia seemed to have a fairly good understanding of what was happening and had done an admirable job being the "big sister" to three-year-old Syras.

She asked very few questions but didn't shy away from talking about Candace or the latest developments in the case. Cliff and Wilma tried to strike a delicate balance between being truthful and protective of her.

Syras was much more of a mystery. It was nearly impossible to tell how much he was really absorbing, how much he might retain. Cliff and Wilma believed he understood very little.

So it came as quick a shock when they were seated inside a fast-foot restaurant in mid-January, next to a table full of chatty, giggling teenage girls. Syras spent a few moments watching the girls before turning to his parents.

"Candace is lost," he said. "Someone shot her with a gun."

Syras took a sip of his Coke.

Cliff and Wilma exchanged confused looks, wondering where exactly he'd picked up such a story. They tried explaining to Syras that Candace was indeed lost, but nobody knew what happened to her.

"That's why we're still looking for her," said Wilma.

. . . .

THURSDAY JANUARY 17, 1985

There was a fine line between suspicion and paranoia. On this day, Wilma wasn't sure exactly what she was feeling.

She was coming off yet another sleepless night, this time consumed by the theory that someone they knew could have harmed Candace.

Wilma was particularly focused on a neighbour who had walked by their home the previous afternoon. The young man had appeared nervous as he walked by, even more so when he realized Wilma was staring at him through the window. He quickly disappeared from her sight. But he was definitely not out of mind. Wilma spent the rest of the day, and night, thinking about the young man.

Candace had mentioned him before, as someone she wanted nothing to do with. If his name would ever come up around the home, Candace would usually respond with a look of disgust.

Wilma knew that police had already spoken to the man as part of their canvass. He had apparently admitted to being in the neighbourhood around the time Candace vanished but denied any other knowledge.

Wilma had shared her suspicions with Cliff. She suggested they speak to police about the man to ensure he had been properly investigated. Cliff agreed it was a good idea.

He had returned to work at Camp Arnes shortly after Candace had vanished, but would usually only stay for a few hours each day. Wilma had recently joined him in the office, helping organize the summer camp registrations by typing them into the computer. Although it was difficult to concentrate at times, Wilma felt it was good for both of them to get out of the house each day.

Wilma picked him up at Camp Arnes around noon. They stopped to pick up Syras from the babysitter before heading into the police station.

Wilma was anxious to hear what police thought of her newest theory. Perhaps they would suggest trying to trick the man into a confession? Wilma told Cliff they could maybe invite him over, ask him a few questions and maybe catch him in a trap.

They arrived at the police station and stopped at the front desk. The receptionist had an obvious look of surprise when they introduced themselves and asked to speak to the supervisor.

Cliff, Wilma and Syras stood waiting for several minutes before two of the sergeants assigned to Candace's case emerged.

"We just wanted to talk to you for a few minutes about something," said Wilma.

The two officers exchanged nervous glances with each other. They suggested Wilma stay with Syras in the reception area while they spoke with Cliff alone. Wilma wasn't fond of the idea. After all, it was her theory that had brought them down there.

Cliff just shrugged his shoulders.

"It won't take long," he said. Cliff followed the officers into a nearby room. The door was closed behind them.

Wilma sat down in the waiting area. Syras wasn't as patient. He was bouncing off the walls, clearly unhappy to be there. Wilma couldn't blame him, but tried to find a distraction. She leafed through a magazine, showing Syras several pictures of cars. But her real focus remained on the room where Cliff and the officers had gone. They were all still visible through the window.

Wilma was getting upset, her mind racing over what they must be discussing. It appeared to be serious, given the grim looks on all their faces.

After several excruciating minutes, the two officers emerged from the room. Cliff remained behind. One of the officers quietly asked the receptionist to keep Syras occupied before inviting Wilma to join them.

"Cliff has something to tell you," they explained.

The officers led Wilma to the office door—then retreated as she walked inside to join her husband.

The door shut behind them.

Cliff was sitting on the edge of a desk. Wilma was thoroughly confused. She sat down on a chair next to her husband. He appeared to be struggling to speak, an anguished look on his tired face.

"Wilma," he began, softly. "They've found Candace. They've found her body … she's dead."

10

Frank Alsip had been buried in paperwork, sorting through various orders and invoices that were gathered on his desk. Construction season was just around the corner. It was Alsip's job to ensure his company –Alsip Brick Tile and Lumber Company—would be ready to meet the demands of its loyal customers.

They were located in the heart of Elmwood, on Cole Avenue in close proximity to the Nairn overpass. It was a large, sprawling property which included the main office, a manufacturing plant and several outlying buildings used mainly for storage.

Alsip glanced up when he heard the front door open. One of his employees, Victor Frankowski, walked in. He looked like he'd just seen a ghost.

"I, uh, think there's a body," Frankowski explained.

Alsip wasn't sure how to react.

Frankowski explained how he'd been out back, looking for a tool, when he checked inside one of the old sheds that was located near the back of the yard.

"Well, we'd better go check," said Alsip.

He followed Frankowski, who was walking quickly. They reached the shed, which included a broken door being held in place with a metal conveyer.

They had brought the shed to Winnipeg from a sand-pit they owned in Beausejour, located just east of the city. It was originally used to store a piece of heavy equipment. Now it sat empty, dormant. It fit in perfectly with some of the other relics in the yard, including several old wagons which the company previously used to deliver material by horseback.

Frankowski stood in front of the shed, explaining how he'd peeked through the opening between the door and the shed on the off chance he might locate a saw he'd been searching for. He stepped aside for Alsip to now do the same.

Alsip was stunned as he looked inside. Frankowski was right.

A body appeared to be lying on the floor. The head was furthest from the door. He couldn't see much else, as the figure appeared to be covered with an old parka that had previously been inside the shed. It was too dark to tell age or gender.

"That definitely looks like a body," said Alsip. "Let's go. We'd better not touch anything."

Alsip and Frankowski returned to the office and immediately called 911.

....

"Cliff, don't joke about this."

Wilma Derksen refused to believe what her husband had just told her. She was already angry at police for speaking to Cliff alone. Now she believed they must have confused him about what was happening with the investigation.

"I'm not joking, Wilma," Cliff said.

"You don't come to the police station on your own and then hear this. It's too outlandish," Wilma insisted.

"They've been trying to get hold of us," said Cliff.

None of this made any sense.

"Dead?" Wilma asked.

"Yes," Cliff said. "She was found in a shack by the Nairn overpass."

"That close?" said Wilma. "When did they find her?"

"This morning," Cliff replied.

Wilma paused, a million emotions running through her body at once. None of this seemed real.

"How ... did she die?" she asked.

"They don't know yet," Cliff said, hesitating. "Her hands and feet were tied. It looks like she froze to death."

"Her hands and feet were tied!" Wilma repeated. Tears began flowing. Breathing now seemed like a struggle.

Cliff was crying as well.

"How do they know it's Candace?" she asked.

"They want me to identify her," said Cliff.

"I'm going with you," Wilma replied.

In many ways, this was the moment Wilma had been expecting. But this wasn't the way she figured it would go down. Wilma thought the grim news would be delivered by police officers who arrived at her door, perhaps in the middle of the night.

"Then it's all over," Wilma said.

They stepped out of the office and were met by the two police sergeants who had been pacing nervously outside. They offered to drive Wilma and Syras home, allowing Cliff to go to the hospital.

Syras ran over to his parents. It was clear he was frightened, but had no idea what was happening. He grabbed Wilma's hand tightly.

Wilma explained she didn't just want to see Candace—she HAD to see her.

Cliff said he would drive.

....

"I'm scared, Cliff."

The drive to Seven Oaks Hospital seemed to be taking forever. But in many ways, Wilma wanted it that way. She didn't know how she could face what was waiting for her.

"Cliff, how are we going to through with this? What if it's too horrible to bear?"

Police had told Cliff there didn't appear to be any physical injuries on Candace.

"We have to remember that she isn't suffering any-more," Cliff said soothingly.

Wilma knew this was true. They would only be viewing Candace's body. They knew she was safe now, in heaven.

....

Several officers from the Winnipeg police homicide unit were already at the hospital when the Derksens entered a private a lounge. The investigators expressed their condo-lences and promised they would do everything they could to find out what happened. Then they handed a pair of Polaroid pictures to Cliff and Wilma.

"She doesn't look pretty," one of the officers warned. "The blotches on her skin are from the cold. They aren't bruises."

Cliff and Wilma took a quick look at the images. It was worst moment of their lives. Their beautiful, precious daughter looked just as Wilma had feared—it seemed like the horror of facing death appeared to be etched on her face.

"I'm so sorry," one of the investigators said. "We thought showing pictures would help to prepare you."

Police explained how the autopsy would have to wait until Candace's body had thawed.

Wilma repeatedly asked how her daughter had died.

"It doesn't make sense. What would be the motive? Who would just take her and just tie her up and leave her to die? She didn't have any enemies," said Wilma.

"It could have been sex. Tying ... bondage ... it's sexual," an officer replied.

His answer cut like a knife.

"All of this is a little hard to believe," Wilma said.

Syras had been taken to another room, away from the raw emotion of the moment.

It was time to go see Candace.

....

A tiny figure lay draped with a white sheet on what appeared to be an operating table.

It wasn't Candace. In real life Candace was so much bigger. This was just a little corpse.

But I forced myself to look closer.

Yes, it was Candace.

Candace minus her personality was so small, so terribly small, just a shell.

Frozen, she looked like a grotesque, dusty mannequin, and I drew back in horror. I didn't feel any attachment to what lay there.

It was Candace's body, but it wasn't Candace.

....

One of the biggest homicide investigations in Winnipeg's history was now underway. Police had quickly sealed off Alsip's entire property and would remain on scene for several days. No stone would be left unturned.

Statements were taken from Frank Alsip and Victor Frankowski. The pair repeatedly went through every detail of the shocking discovery. Neither of them recalled seeing anything suspicious over the past several weeks.

They were especially surprised to learn Candace Derksen was inside the shed, considering police had actually searched their property during the last big investigative push on December 30th.

Police were just as confused, conceding the shed must have somehow been overlooked by investigators that day.

Robert Parker had been dispatched to the scene, knowing he was likely wading into one of the most important cases of his career. As a constable in the identification unit, it was Parker's job to methodically document every piece of evidence.

He was 11 years into the job, the past seven as a specialist in crime scene photography. Parker had also been trained through the Canadian Police College in the ever-emerging field of seizing and preserving exhibits for future examination.

Parker had arrived just after 10:15 a.m. and headed straight for the shed. His supervising sergeant, Wayne Bellingham, was already on scene. Parker documented the removal of Candace's body, snapping several photos of where she was originally located. Winnipeg First Call, a local mortuary service, had been tasked with transporting the body to hospital.

Parker's main duty on this day was to stay with the body. He followed Candace to the hospital, waited while her family identified her, and then began the unenviable task of photographing the entire process leading up to, and including, her eventual autopsy.

He documented all of the items of clothing she was wearing—the blue and burgundy winter jacket, the blue hooded sweatshirt, the blue jeans with stains on the knees, the white socks—and one shoe.

Her right shoe was missing. However, the rest of her clothing appeared in normal condition. There was no evidence anything else had been removed or tampered with.

Parker also watched as members of the homicide unit collected the exhibits—which included a white metal ring with a blue heart-shaped stone found in her jean pockets, along with a rubber band and gum wrapper.

Candace's body was eventually covered with a white sheet. The bindings around her arms remained in place. They wouldn't be removed until her autopsy was held three days later.

....

The phone was ringing off the hook and friends began arriving at their door. Candace Derksen's death was all over the news.

Cliff and Wilma had driven home in mostly stunned silence, a mixture of relief and agony.

Their first visitor had been a newspaper reporter, asking the obligatory question of "how are you feeling."

"We're relieved," Wilma said instinctively. "We're glad it's over."

Cliff was standing nearby.

"In many ways it is over," he began. "But in many ways it is just beginning."

Once the reporter had left, Wilma turned to her husband.

"What do you mean it isn't over yet?" she asked.

"We have to find the killer now," said Cliff.

....

The next several hours were a blur. Cliff had gone to pick Odia up from school, fearing she might hear the news second-hand once it began filtering through the community.

The Derksen home was quickly filled with loved ones who began handling the media inquiries, putting up a protective wall for Cliff and Wilma. There were plenty of cups of hot tea, many tears and countless prayers. Several of Candace's friends, including Heidi Harms and David Wiebe, also stopped by along with their parents. Everyone was in shock. They all needed each other right now.

They received an unexpected visit from the father of Barbara Stoppel, a 16-year-old Winnipeg girl who had been strangled while working in a donut shop back in 1981. Her killing was one of the most notorious in the city's history. Now Barbara's family was reaching out to Candace's.

It was after midnight when the last of the guests had left. Others, like Heidi and her mother, were spending the night in the basement.

It had taken longer than usual to settle Syras and Odia was taking the news of Candace's death especially hard. Cliff and Wilma knew the coming days were going to be extremely difficult as reality set it.

The couple was getting ready for bed, physically exhausted and emotionally spent. Neither had any idea how to go forward from here. There was no textbook, no blueprint on how to cope with such a tragedy. All they had was each other, along with a huge network of supporters.

"Cliff, do you think we're going to lose everything?" Wilma whispered to her husband in the quiet of their own bedroom. She was well aware of studies which spoke of increased risk of divorce among parents of slain children. "There has to be a way around this. I don't want to lose everything," she continued.

"We won't," Cliff said.

"But how can we be certain? Cliff, I don't want to lose you, the kids, my health or my sanity. We've made it this far. We have to make it," said Wilma.

She finished brushing her teeth, her mind focused on Cliff's comments to the reporter earlier that day about this just being the beginning in many ways. She was also thinking about the words of wisdom offered by Barbara Stoppel's loved ones.

"Cliff. I think he [Mr. Stoppel] came to tell us that if we look for justice it will destroy us," Wilma said as she climbed into bed. Cliff was sitting on the edge of the bed, pulling off his socks. He remained silent.

"Cliff, I don't think we are ever going to find a justice that will truly satisfy us by trying to find the murderer or seeing if he gets what he deserves. I think we have to find it another way," said Wilma.

She continued, "We will have to wait for true justice. We won't find it here on Earth."

Cliff reached over to turn off the lights.

"We won't be able to figure it all out tonight, sweets," he said.

11

"Do you see her?"

Wilma Derksen had been fighting sleep for what seemed like hours. Every attempt to close her eyes would trigger a fast-moving collage of images that would take her from the police station to the morgue. She could sense her husband was facing a similar struggle.

"Yes,". Cliff replied. "I can't get her face out of my mind."

Several minutes of painful silence followed. One of the most difficult things to grasp was the fact Candace had been found only about 500 metres from their home.

"Let's remember pictures of Candace when she was a baby," Wilma finally suggested. She thought happy memories might bring them some comfort now as they lay in bed, facing their fears in the dark of night.

"I remember her in a yellow snowsuit, just learning to walk," Wilma began.

"Candace in a dark navy pantsuit in the autumn leaves," Cliff offered.

"The birthday picture where she put the spoon in her mouth and wouldn't take a bite because the movie camera was running," said Wilma.

They continued this game for several minutes, neither one wanting to stop. It was all they could do to keep that horrific final image of Candace out of their heads.

....

FRIDAY JANUARY 18, 1985

They had worked tirelessly for weeks, hoping for a happy ending to a heartbreaking situation. So news that Candace Derksen's body had been found cast a pall over the regularly scheduled meeting of the civilian search committee formed in her name.

Cliff and Wilma insisted on attending, wanting to personally thank everyone who had dedicated their time and effort. The couple had spent their morning meeting with Klassen's Funeral Home to discuss details of Candace's burial. It was an emotional few hours, filled with questions about plots and cemeteries and guest lists and coffins that were difficult to answer in their grief.

They had selected a small white casket—then agreed to purchase a cement vault which would surround the coffin and keep the ground from caving in around it. Cliff had insisted, despite his wife's hesitation because of the extra cost.

"I couldn't protect her during life. I want to protect her now," Cliff said, with tears streaming down his face.

Walter Klassen, the funeral director, cried along with them.

"I never really get used to it," he said.

Now at the meeting, members of the search committee insisted on covering all costs of the funeral through the money they had raised.

Candace's body likely wouldn't be released for several days, so it was decided to hold the funeral on January 24th.

There was also discussion about finding a way to carry on Candace's name. Cliff and Wilma suggested a Memorial Fund, which could ultimately contribute to a new swimming pool at Camp Arnes. Candace loved being in the water and everyone agreed it was a perfect way to honour her.

"Swimming was our regular Saturday night activity that drew us together so much as a family," said Cliff.

Other topics included discussion of how students at MBCI would be offered grief counselling. There was also agreement to hold a news conference the following day in which Cliff and Wilma would speak to the media. The meeting ended just as it began—with prayers.

....

Candace Derksen's classmates left Mennonite Brethren Collegiate in tears after being told by teachers she had been found dead.

"We never thought it would happen to our best friend," Jennifer Wedel, Grade 7, said sobbing. "Now my dad drives me to school."

Principal Harry Wall and Vice-principal Dave Teigrob visited the classroom about 3:30 p.m. Thursday to break the tragic news.

"We just told them very plainly and simply that they had found Candace's body and to pray for the family," Wall said.

Wall said he repeated earlier warnings for students not to go anywhere alone.

"Now everybody's really scared," Michelle Mourre, 12, another close friend of Derksen, said.

Mourre said Derksen was the last person she would have expected to go with a stranger anywhere. She said she hasn't gone to the bus without a companion since Derksen's disappearance Nov. 30.

"It's kind of scary. It's like a bomb dropping," Nina Zandstra said, adding students were dismissed after the announcement.

Mourre said the news brought her classmates closer together.

"Everybody needs each other the most now," Mourre said. "Everybody was crying. They didn't care who saw."

Bonnie Toews, 16, who coached Derksen's volleyball team, said: "I was always scared that would be what happened."

River East school trustee Helen Mayba said she's noticed more parents driving their children home since the search for Candace began.

Teigrob, also the school's student counsellor, said he would try to discuss Derksen's death with students during the next few days to let them voice their concerns.

"It will take time for them to work it through," Teigrob said. "It's a tragic event—a reflection of the evil in our society."

—*WINNIPEG FREE PRESS*, FRIDAY JANUARY 18, 1985

....

Winnipeg police were being flooded with media queries about their ongoing homicide investigation. There was little to say publicly—and investigators weren't about to tip their hand while the search for a killer was underway.

"We're playing our cards close to the vest right now," Crime Supt. Des Depourcq told reporters. In reality, they were dealing with a pretty thin deck.

Police were hit with several questions about how they could have missed Candace's body during the search of Alsip's property on December 30th. There was no clear answer, other than a simple oversight.

"I can't remember why it wasn't checked, but it wasn't. It's one of a dozen buildings I've got here," Frank Alsip told reporters. "Nobody ever thought anything of that damn building."

Privately, police told the Derksen family they believed an officer took a quick look inside the shed but didn't see anything. They noted it had been a bright sunny day and the glare off the snow may have made it difficult for the officer to see anything inside the small, dark shed.

At least a dozen officers had now been assigned to the case full-time. A grieving family and a shaken community were counting on them.

....

SATURDAY JANUARY 19, 1985

"We would have hoped that the occasion that would bring us together again would be a happier one than this."

Harold Jantz began the highly-anticipated news conference by speaking to a throng of reporters from a carefully prepared statement. He wanted to say a few words on behalf of the search committee. Cliff and Wilma stood at his side.

"Our hope and prayer was that Candace could be returned to her family alive. At the same time, we were fully aware of the possibility that she might not be found alive. We have had to face the reality that we live in a small world in which people do terrible things to one another, and that death is always possible. Nevertheless, faith in God and the knowledge that ultimately nothing could separate Candace from the love of God has given the Derksens and the church community of which they are a part, courage and comfort and peace as the possibility of Candace's murder became a reality."

Jantz also thanked the media and police investigators for their role in the case.

"We have sensed from police that their concern was more than professional. They felt the pain too as human beings and as family people," he said.

Jantz stepped aside and turned the podium over to Cliff and Wilma.

....

It was a question they had expected would be asked.

"How do you feel about whoever did this to Candace?"

Cliff and Wilma didn't hesitate with their answer—even though they both knew it would likely leave some people scratching their heads.

"We would like to know who the person or persons are so we could share, hopefully, a love that seems to be missing in these people's lives," Cliff replied. "I don't believe the person who did this had loving parents or a circle of friends who thought the world of him or he wouldn't have done a deed like this."

Wilma felt much the same way, knowing their Mennonite faith was the foundation of how they lived their lives. Now was not the time to abandon their belief system. It was a time to embrace it. And with faith came forgiveness, even if it seemed like a difficult concept to grasp at this time.

"Our main concern was to find Candace. We've found her. The rest is up to police. I can't say at this point I forgive this person, but we all have done something dreadful in our lives or we have the urge to," said Wilma.

The questions kept coming.

"What are your views on the death penalty?"

Cliff maintained a calm, steady demeanour.

"I'm not sure I want to get into an issue like that right now. I feel it is important that this person or persons be taken off the streets so they don't hurt anyone else. Our personal interest would be to rehabilitate this person," he said.

Wilma repeatedly thanked the community and the countless volunteers who had worked so hard to find Candace. She discussed their hopes of carrying on their daughter's legacy through a variety of projects, including the creation of a Child Find chapter in Winnipeg to help other families who lost a loved one. Plans were also announced for the creation of the Memorial Fund in

Candace's name, which would eventually go towards a swimming pool at Camp Arnes.

"We can turn this into something good," said Wilma, noting nearly 1,200 children attend Arnes summer camp every year.

"It was our dream that Camp Arnes build a swimming pool. Here families and their children could spend time together loving one another, and growing closer together, building character in a healthy camping atmosphere," Cliff explained. "Candace loved Camp Arnes and made some key life decisions while she was at camp. This tragic event has also made Wilma and myself more determined than ever to work with children and families, building wholesome personalities, giving love, teaching how to love, building and strengthening the family unit. If men and women today knew that they were loved and appreciated we wouldn't have the people in our society who have to do such horrible things to fulfill the lack they are experiencing."

Wilma also extended an open invitation to anyone who wished to attend Candace's funeral, which would be held at the 1,000 seat Mennonite Brethren Church on Portage Avenue instead of the family's much smaller personal church.

"We are certainly welcoming the public. We're aware very many people have become part of this search for Candace so we know many will be interested in attending."

One of the final questions concerned the Winnipeg Police Service and whether there were any hard feelings, especially since it was now apparent they somehow missed finding Candace during the December 30th search which included Alsip's property.

"It's a disappointment she wasn't found then, but then we are always wiser in hindsight. We don't hold any antagonism against the police. Maybe if they didn't act on information it would be different. But they did act right away," said Cliff. "It's a tremendous relief knowing where Candace is. We have found Candace unfortunately not alive. It's a tragedy she had to die such a violent death. We can grieve in peace now."

....

TUESDAY JANUARY 22, 1985

A tragedy that had brought out the best in so many people had, unfortunately, unearthed a few loose cannons. Like the woman who called the Derksen residence to give them an earful about the way they were handling their grief.

"I'm going to protest the funeral," she vowed.

The information was passed on to the civilian search committee, which was holding one of their final meetings before dissolving.

Police had been notified of the woman's threat and promised to have a presence at the funeral in case anyone tried to start trouble. As well, police promised to pay special attention to the Derksen residence while they were at the church service and cemetery.

Heartless thieves had been known in the past to scour the obituaries and take advantage of families they knew would be away. The fact Candace's funeral was such a high-profile event only increased the likelihood.

Mayor Bill Norrie was going to attend the service, along with at least half a dozen members of the police service who simply wanted to pay their respects.

A large entourage of staff from Camp Arnes would also be attending. There were also 15 out-of-town relatives from both Cliff and Wilma's family that were coming in for the service. They would attend a private family viewing later that evening, which would include an open casket.

"It's a miracle that after six weeks we can still see her one last time. It's truly a gift," Wilma's mother had said repeatedly.

Police would provide an escort from the church to Glen Eden cemetery, which would be Candace's final resting place. There were also plans by police to unveil a Crime Stoppers campaign in the next few weeks that would portray Candace's case.

The committee also had an internal debate about the $2,000 reward they had offered for information leading to Candace. Committee members agreed the money should go to Victor Frankowski, the Alsip's employee who discovered her body in the shed.

"The reward didn't have anything to do with the apprehension of the suspect," said Harold Jantz.

But Frankowski apparently wasn't interested. He was still reeling over his tragic find and wasn't looking to profit from it.

"I don't think he feels he should take it. I don't think he would feel he deserved it," his wife, Raeleen, explained.

....

The family, and committee, had just received the preliminary autopsy results. Dr. Peter Markesteyn, the chief medical examiner for Manitoba, concluded Candace died of
exposure to the harsh winter elements. He believed it
was likely a quick death, perhaps within a few hours of
her disappearance.

There were no visible signs of abuse, save for the
restraints which would have made it difficult for Candace
to escape the shed. However, those results only raised
more questions about a potential motive.

And they were seemingly no closer to catching the killer.

....

WEDNESDAY JANUARY 23, 1985
They were less than 24 hours away from burying their
daughter. But Winnipeg police wanted a few minutes of
their time.

"Can't it wait until after the funeral?" Cliff had asked.
Police said it couldn't.

"Can you come to our house? It would make it easier."
Cliff continued. Police said they couldn't. They insisted
there was nothing to be concerned about, they just wanted to complete a formal statement that was routine in
these types of investigation.

Despite a house full of out-of-town guests, Cliff and
Wilma made the short drive to the police station. Their
statements would be taken separately—a process that
was again explained as routine.

Wilma went first. She sat down with two homicide
sergeants in a small room and began facing a series of

rapid-fire questions. It wasn't long before a pattern began to emerge. They all seemed to be about Cliff.

"How often did he go look for Candace?" they asked.

Wilma said she couldn't remember.

"Try," they insisted.

Wilma began thinking out loud.

"At least twice," she said.

"For how long?" police asked.

"Not long. Maybe he went three times. He must have gone three times," Wilma said.

She was quite concerned about where this conversation appeared to be heading.

"What times did he leave?" police asked.

"When did he return?"

The questions seemed to be repeating themselves. It felt like an interrogation. Could they possibly suspect Cliff had something to do with Candace's death?

12

I was grateful for the storm. It was a gift. It would have been so much harder if it had been a nice day with the birds singing in the trees. Somehow this strange storm was a reflection of our inner turmoil: no one has the right to take another person's life; the world is a cruel unfriendly place where innocent children have to absorb the pain; since the creation, everything has gone wrong; we are spinning out of control.

....

THURSDAY JANUARY 24, 1985

They had packed one of Winnipeg's largest places of worship on a bitterly cold day, braving a strong north wind and biting wind chill to say goodbye to a young girl who had captured their hearts. More than 1,500 people crammed inside Mennonite Brethren Church—at least 300 of them forced to watch the service on video monitors set up in the basement.

Cliff, Wilma, Syras and Odia had been picked up by a black limousine from the funeral home early in the morning, leading a procession of vehicles which included other family members to the Portage Avenue congregation.

They had left their home in the guard of two police detectives. There would be other undercover officers at the funeral, scouring the crowd for faces. Cliff and Wilma had been told this was a routine investigative technique, as killers sometimes attend the services for their victims. This didn't frighten the couple. In fact, they hoped Candace's killer would attend, if only to see the outpouring of love and support for his victim.

The Derksens entered the crowded church, where Candace's small white coffin sat covered with red roses at the front. A banner, with the words "Friends Are Friends Forever", was also draped over the casket.

Wilma looked over to the Mennonite Brethren school choir and smiled at David Wiebe and several other students she recognized. A large throng of media was seated near the front.

"Cliff and Wilma are overwhelmed that so many of you have come from all over the city to share their sorrow," Pastor Keith Poysti said to begin the service.

Wilma was overcome with emotion, unable to sing the words to the opening hymn, *We Praise Thee, O God*. She scanned the crowd, amazed to see so many friends and even more strangers. They were here for Candace.

Dave Loewen was the first to speak, bringing words of comfort and condolence on behalf of the civilian search committee.

"By God's hand, Candace has become a sacrificial lamb. This event has brought into focus both the worst and the best of Winnipeg. While evil has run its course, good has triumphed," said Loewen.

The choir sang another hymn. Ruth Balzer, who had worked with Candace thought a winter program at Camp Arnes, was the next to talk.

"To know Candace was to love her, not because she was more special than anyone else, but because she knew how to love," Balzer said. "I often saw her draw out a shy person or make a newcomer feel welcome. She is an example of what it is to love and to care."

Balzer told a story of how Candace cherished a worn, tarnished locket which had been given to her at the age of eight by her family. Although she had received other necklaces over the years, Candace always went back to the same locket.

Wilma shuddered. Candace had been wearing the locket the day she vanished. The memento was recovered with her body, found inside her pocket.

Another hymn followed. Wilma was in awe at the beautiful sounds filling the church.

Cliff was now up. He thanked everyone for coming and shared details of the Memorial Fund. He choked back tears describing his daughter's love of swimming, family and community. And then he introduced her favourite song, which began playing over the church speakers.

> With the faith and love God's given
> Springing from the hope we know
> We will pray the joy you live in
> In the strength that now you show
> But we'll keep you close as always
> It won't even seem you're gone
> 'Cause our hearts in big and small ways

Will keep the love that keeps us strong
And friends are friends forever
If the Lord's the Lord of them
And a friend will not say "never"
'Cause the welcome will not end.
Thought it's hard to let you go
In the Father's hands we know
That a lifetime's not too long to live as friends.

....

Pastor John Epp was the last to speak. He said the Derksen family had suffered a tremendous loss.

"Their life in this world will never be complete again as it was with Candace. No one can fill her place. It belongs to her," said Epp.

He said an even greater tragedy than Candace's death is the fact someone caused it.

"There is someone, one or more, unknown to us as yet and who, for reasons unknown, executed violence against Candace," said Epp.

He urged everyone to search for the killer with "forgiveness and love in their hearts."

"Something in him is more dead than Candace. Whether he knows it or not, his life needs love and wholeness," he said.

....

The service ended with another of Candace's favourite songs, called "Great Is The Lord."

As she listened to the soothing words, Wilma recalled a conversation she once had with her daughter.

"Mom, my favourite song is *Friends Are Friends Forever*, and I wanted to tape only that one, but I accidentally taped *Great Is The Lord* as well, and now I keep listening to it, too. I almost like it as much. *Friends* makes me a little sad. *Great Is The Lord* picks me up and leaves me with a good feeling."

Now the entire Derksen family was following Candace's casket down the aisle as the choir sang along.

> Great are you Lord
> and worthy of Glory.
> Great are you Lord
> and worthy of praise.
> I lift up my voice
> I lift up my voice
> Great are you Lord.

. . . .

They stepped outside the church, the early-morning sun now replaced with dark clouds. Snow had started falling. The temperature was dropping fast.

The Derksens climbed back inside the black limousine, beginning a long, slow-moving procession down Portage Avenue towards the cemetery. Visibility was severely reduced. The storm was getting worse as they hit the northern outskirts of Winnipeg, where Glen Eden was located.

They gathered around the gravesite for a brief ceremony. Pastors Epp and Poysti offered a few final prayers as Candace's coffin was lowered into the ground. The air was biting, yet Wilma wished she could remove her winter jacket. She wanted to feel the same cold Candace had felt in her final moments alive.

The funeral director handed each family member a flower. Wilma was the last to place it on the coffin, which was ice cold to the touch.

"Bye, Candace. I love you," she whispered.

....

The strength and faith of the Derksen family through their terrible ordeal has been a source of inspiration for many Winnipeggers.

It is difficult to believe that anything positive could come from such a tragedy, yet the Derksens have asked us to believe that all along.

Even skeptics have found that the family is right. There is a positive side to this heart-rending story. It is the capacity of human beings to draw close when some among us are in trouble.

It is the story of human need answered by human fortitude. It is the emotion we have all felt throughout these eight weeks: empathy for the family's loss, tears at the final terrible discovery that Candace was dead, and finally admiration for people whose convictions prove stronger than the base animal instincts of those who took Candace from the world.

Pull together, Winnipeg. Help this heroic family in its struggle to understand this senseless crime.

It makes us all better people.

—*WINNIPEG SUN* EDITORIAL, FRIDAY JANUARY 25, 1985

....

The search for Candace was over—but the civilian committee which had been formed in her name was continuing to press on with their work. Two major issues remained. More than $15,000 had been raised for the Memorial Fund in just a few short weeks. Donations were pouring in from everywhere. The most touching example was a young girl who pooled together her penny collection and brought in $28.87 in copper. The total had been boosted by adding the $2,000 which had been earmarked for a reward, yet turned down by the man who found Candace's body.

However, the City of Winnipeg was planning on issuing a $5,000 reward for information leading to the arrest of the person responsible for her killing. A major Crime Stoppers campaign was going to be launched in March. In their final meeting, the search committee voted to turn the funds over to Camp Arnes for the pool which would be constructed in her name.

The creation of a Child Find chapter in Manitoba was also close to becoming a reality. Wilma Derksen had agreed to sit on a board of directors, along with prominent local businessman Len DeFehr and Ester DeFehr. The group had ambitious plans to network with parents across the province that were experiencing the grief and anguish of having a child go missing.

The Derksens attended the final meeting to formally thank the committee for all the work they had done.

"Words really can't express how we feel. Just let us assure you again that we'll never forget what you have done for us. We will always be indebted to you for the time you spent, your expertise, your understanding, your faith and your prayers," said Wilma. "You showed how important a life is and how powerful love is."

....

The final autopsy results were in. But they offered little comfort and even fewer answers. Police stopped by the Derksens home to report toxicology tests showed Candace hadn't been drugged or poisoned.

"Was she sexually assaulted?" Wilma asked. She braced herself for the reply.

"No," police said.

"Was she hurt in any way?"

Police explained that Candace likely died quickly. Her vocal chords weren't swollen—indicating she hadn't attempted to scream.

"It doesn't look as if she struggled much," one of the investigators told the family. This led police to make an assumption.

"Because of this evidence, she was probably with someone she knew," they said.

Wilma was confused. She felt her stomach sink as she thought back to the bizarre conversation in the police station the day before the funeral, in which investigators seemed especially interested in Cliff.

Police seemed to interpret a lack of screaming and struggling as meaning there must have been no fear. And, therefore, a connection with the killer. They also explained the scene inside the shed was disorganized, indicating her attacker may have either been in a hurry or perhaps careless. They expressed confidence they would find the person who was responsible. And fast.

As police were leaving, the one of the investigators turned to Wilma and uttered one final piece of information. It was as if the officer had read her mind.

"She was a virgin," he said.

It confirmed everything Wilma had believed about her daughter.

She really had been an innocent little girl—half woman, half child—who had been lured or forced off the street that night and terrorized, Wilma thought to herself.

....

Wilma had lost more than 15 pounds. Cliff's hair had greyed. Both had learned to function—or at least give the appearance of functioning—on just a few hours of sleep a night. The past few months had taken a heavy toll on the couple. But now, as they adjusted to a new normal, they were taking some time to reflect on all that had happened.

Cliff and Wilma often spent their evenings poring through piles of letters they had received, mostly from strangers offering words of support.

"During the time Candace was missing and after she was found, I seemed to be fighting with God. I couldn't see why he took her life away, why it had to be Candace. She was a Christian and a darn good one. How could He let this happen to her and us?" one teenage girl wrote.

"I love Candace as a fellow human being and I would like to aspire to be more like her—to be able to love and care as much as she did. I've cried a lot over this," a devoutly religious young man said in his note to the family.

There were even letters sent from Stony Mountain penitentiary, the medium-security federal prison just north of Winnipeg.

"My greatest and deepest apology for your dear daughter. I'm a prisoner convicted of murder," wrote one inmate.

There were letters from other grieving parents, letters and drawings from young children, and condolences sent directly from Prime Minister Brian Mulroney.

Cliff and Wilma were replying to as many of the notes as they could, wanting to thank everyone for their support and wisdom. They also penned a letter which was published in their weekly church bulletin. It read as follows:

Dear Brothers and Sisters in Christ,

We have just completed the two most difficult months in our lives, and we just want to thank you for being with us.

Now it just seems like a dreadful nightmare, except that we have an empty chair at our kitchen table as a painful reminder that it was a reality. We know that we could never have survived the ordeal without you.

Even though we were often absorbed in our hurt and not always aware of what was happening around us, we were always conscious of being ministered to and being taken care of. In many ways it was like a hospital experience. Suffering from shock and enveloped in our own world of pain, we were still aware of people much like nurses and doctors coming and going, checking our temperature, reassuring us that we'd make it, giving nourishment, decorating our place with cards and flowers, giving us Bible verses when we couldn't concentrate enough to read for ourselves, praying for us when we couldn't find the words and giving us advice and direction when we couldn't see the way. What continually amazed us was how well the care was organized. There was always someone there when we needed them. We entertained so many angels unawares.

Now we think it a privilege to have seen God's body at work. We saw how every person in the Christian community has a unique gift. When meals arrived at our house they weren't all lasagna (not that we would have minded) but everyone brought something different. We didn't receive ten Christmas trees, we only received one. Our freezer had an assortment of goodies that we couldn't have planned better. Visitors didn't come all at once. Those that could write wrote beautiful letters. Those that prayed, prayed. Those that had, gave financially. And those who were gifted with words of comfort, counselled. Some cleaned, some shopped, some organized, some babysat, some screened telephone calls. For whatever need we had there seemed to be someone with a gift to fill it.

We only regret that much of the experience is now a bit of a blur and we know that we are not going to be able to thank each of you individually. But feel free to remind us of the part you played in all of this to refresh our memories so we can thank you. And if we still have a dish of yours, please remind us. It will take some time to tie some of these loose ends together.

Thank you for also being so patient with us and for allowing the intrusion of the media into our fellowship. It was a risk we took but now we can see that God has used the exposure for His good. We are just overwhelmed with the letters and the calls from people who have seen your love and faith and now want to find God for themselves.

Nothing is going to replace Candace in our lives. We will have to learn to live with an empty space in our family, but it has helped that we can bandage our hurt with wonderful memories of her love and yours.

God has taught us so much through all of this. We have realized anew that even though God can't spare us from the evil of this world, He can make it bearable by surrounding us with his love and the love and support of His children.

As the verse in Psalms 32:10 says: "The Lord's unfailing love surrounds those who trust in Him."

Thank you for being there when we needed you and we hope to be there when you need us.

In His love,
Cliff and Wilma Derksen.

....

Not surprisingly, the Derksens were also receiving letters people taking issue with their very public position on tolerance on forgiveness.

"I still do not understand how you can send out precious love for the killer of Candace? He/she has stolen something very precious from you and you send out love? In the Bible doesn't it say 'EYE FOR EYE, TOOTH FOR TOOTH.' I feel much hatred for that person and cannot forgive what he has done to a sweet, innocent thirteen-year-old girl. I do not understand your feelings," one stranger wrote.

There were a handful of others expressing similar sentiments.

Cliff was very much at ease with his position, while Wilma found herself struggling with the issue at times. One prime example came during a coffee date with a concerned old friend.

"If you could let yourself go, what would satisfy justice for you? Would it be execution?" the woman asked.

Wilma initially shot down the suggestion, explaining how that would make her no better than the killer. But what came out of her mouth next shocked her.

"His death ... one death ... wouldn't satisfy me," Wilma said, the hesitation very much apparent. "Ten child murderers would have to die."

Wilma closed her eyes, picturing a scenario of 10 hooded figures up against a wall as she walked towards them, a gun in her hand, and began pulling the trigger. A few seconds of unadulterated glee were quickly pushed aside by pangs of guilt and instant remorse.

"But that doesn't satisfy," she concluded. "I think our choice to forgive is the right one."

Wilma had temporarily lost control, allowed herself to be consumed by a rage she didn't even realize existed. She vowed never to let it happen again.

13

It's one thing to be suspected of being an unkind or inept parent; it's another thing completely to be suspected of murder. Were we now murder suspects? Was that the change we were feeling? I shoved the thought aside. That was ridiculous. We had good alibis: I had been home with the kids; Cliff had been at the office. There was no way that we could have been involved.

There were so many possible scenarios. Had someone intended to sexually assault Candace but, because of my prayers, suddenly decided not to do it? Had there been a noise outside the shed that had frightened him off? Had Candace said something that miraculously turned him off?

....

Lily Loewen, the outdoor education coordinator, had stopped by Wilma Derksen's desk and delivered a bombshell.

"There are vicious rumours," she said.

Wilma figured she knew where this was heading.

"We've heard them all by now. Are Cliff and I divorcing again?" Wilma said with a chuckle.

Loewen shook her head in the negative, a serious look on her face.

"Candace was illegitimate? I had an affair with the milkman? Or maybe it was the mailman this time," Wilma continued, laughing.

"No," Loewen replied.

"Well then, what have we done now? Let me in on the gossip," said Wilma.

Loewen hesitated.

"Lily, we've been through the worst. It really doesn't matter what people are saying. It's never going to be as painful as losing Candace. You can tell me. I can deal with things," Wilma said,

Loewen still didn't seem convinced. Finally she broke her silence, tears streaming from her eyes.

"Wilma, they are accusing Cliff of killing Candace."

Wilma was stunned.

Loewen said how there were rumblings within the community that police were focusing on Cliff as their prime suspect. Wilma instantly flashed back to the police interview room, fending off accusatory questions from investigators.

"But they know Cliff was at the office. They couldn't possibly. If anyone has an alibi, it's Cliff," Wilma said.

"They think it is entirely possible that after you picked up Cliff and he went looking for Candace, he might have found her in a compromising situation and taken her to the shack and left her there as punishment. Later he went back, and she was dead," Loewen explained.

Wilma couldn't believe what she was hearing.

"But Cliff isn't like that. When he went looking the first time, we were already scared. To find her in any kind of situation would have been a relief," said Wilma.

"I know," said Loewen.

The conversation continued for several minutes. Wilma found herself increasingly angry—not at her co-worker, but for anyone who could think her husband could have done such a thing. Wilma knew how much Candace's disappearance had devastated Cliff. There was absolutely no way he could be involved.

No way.

Wilma wasn't sure how to explain this to Cliff, but knew she couldn't keep him in the dark about what people were apparently whispering behind his back. She finally worked up the courage to tell him two nights later, as they poured a cup of tea after Odia and Syras had gone to sleep. Cliff was mortified.

Days later, police called the Derksen home with a request.

"We'd like Cliff to come down to the station and take a polygraph test."

....

The rumour mill was seemingly working overtime, as David Wiebe's name also continued to surface in water-cooler gossip. There were whispers that the older boy who had eyes for Candace may have been involved. Or perhaps it had been a continuation of the school-yard snowball hijinks gone horribly wrong.

Police held a news conference in March, announcing their Crime Stoppers campaign to catch Candace's killer. One of the officers had explained the working theory.

"The motive may not have started off as murder. It may have started off as an innocent event," he said.

A reporter asked if it could have been a childish prank turned tragedy.

"That's what I'm leading to," the officer replied.

....

It wasn't just the Derksen family that was desperately waiting for answers from police. Members of the public were flooding open-line radio talk shows and penning letters-to-the-editor demanding more information about the investigation. The media soon joined the chorus, as illustrated by a strongly-worded column in the *Winnipeg Free Press* written by Barry Mullin.

> Few murder cases in Winnipeg history have created more community concern and public participation than that of Candace Wynne Derksen.
>
> Candace, 13, disappeared about 4:15 p.m. Nov. 30, after she called home from a corner store near Mennonite Brethren Collegiate Institute.
>
> A Grade 7 student at MBCI, Candace wanted a ride home. Her mother was busy and told her daughter she'd have to make the 15-minute walk home alone.
>
> Candace's disappearance triggered a community alert.
>
> Rewards were offered, neighbourhoods searched and fellow students went door-to-door to search and distribute posters asking for help in locating the missing girl.
>
> Candace's body was discovered Jan. 17 in a plywood shack in a little-used industrial lumber yard 500 metres from her home.

In the time since her bound, fully-clothed body was found by the yard foreman, police have provided few details concerning Candace's death.

Unanswered questions have fuelled vivid imaginations: speculations of circumstance and possible motive have heightened public fear in city neighbourhoods.

Parents use the case to warn sons and daughters about perceived dangers. Many Elmwood and East Kildonan parents have taken to driving their children to and from school.

Police crime Supt. Des DePourcq, the man in charge of dispensing details about Candace's death, acknowledges the concerns of the community.

"I just don't know how many mouths are talking or what rumours are flying around," said DePourcq. "But if we try to respond to rumours you get sidetracked on a case and create false issues and that detracts from what you're trying to do—investigate."

Results of an autopsy show that Candace froze to death. Toxicology tests show she wasn't drugged or poisoned. Beyond those facts, DePourcq refuses to discuss details of the case.

"I know that sitting mute on a lot of questions leaves a lot of people wondering, but that's a decision we had to make."

DePourcq has given two reasons for withholding certain facts: police don't want to tip the killer and fewer details help weed out false confessions.

There have been no false confessions in this case, DePourcq said.

As is often the case with high-profile crimes, the question arises of the public's right to certain answers from police, the protectors of the same public.

Police often are eager to ask the news media for help in bringing a specific crime to the attention of the public in the hope the publicity will solve the case. The Crime Stoppers program is a good example of that.

Yet when the media ask tough questions about a murder case which will linger on people's minds, police throw up the excuse of "under investigation."

Police have refused to address too many aspects and questions in this case, including the approximate time of Candace's death; how could searchers have overlooked a body in the small shed; had Candace been sexually assaulted; and was she unconscious when she froze to death?

Answers to those questions surely can't hamper a police investigation.

....

Cliff arrived home shortly after noon. He did not look pleased.

"How did it go?" Wilma asked.

"You're not taking that test," Cliff said sternly. He explained the polygraph examination in detail—how police began with a series of routine questions only to begin throwing direct accusations at him.

Cliff had answered every question directly and honestly, not shying away from anything. When it was over, the polygraph technician took a scan of the results and then turned to him with a smile.

"You are an honest man," he said.

Wilma was thrilled Cliff's name had been cleared. They both hoped police could now spend their precious resources on finding the real culprit. But later that night, in the privacy of her own mind, Wilma found herself struggling to suppress a growing anger towards the police.

They had done nothing but insult us. At first, they had treated us as if we were the abusers. By their insinuations they had called us religious fanatics, unfit parents and alarmists. While Candace had been freezing to death in that shack, they had called her a runaway.

If only they had believed us and gotten out the dogs that night, all this could have been stopped. It was their fault. Their ignorance had prevented us from finding her.

It was personal. They had never listened to me. I had always been treated like an unstable mother, a brainless woman. The day they had found Candace's body, they had kept me waiting in the reception area. They had told my husband before me.

Even worse, they had accused my daughter, who had suffered so much, of being half responsible for what had happened to her. And they had accused my husband of being a murderer. They had suspected all the friends we loved, sometimes even harassed them.

We had tried to be so gracious, and they had shoved it back into our faces.

....

It's amazing what a decent night of sleep—and a little bit of perspective—can do to one's outlook on things. Wilma found this out the following day as she spoke with the distraught father of a young Winnipeg girl who'd gone missing.

She was speaking with the family in her formal capacity as a member of the Child Find board. The family had called, looking for help in tracking down their 17-year-old daughter. They were a Mennonite family living in the city's gritty North End. And they were convinced their daughter had run away.

"Are you sure she ran away?" Wilma asked the father.

He described how the teen had left a note, explaining that was exactly what she planned to do. Wilma began asking a series of additional questions—Why was she upset? What was life at home like? What kind of friends did she have?

It was only later that evening, while driving back to her own home, that Wilma realized exactly what she had done. She had asked many of the same questions police had originally asked her. She had many of the same doubts about the circumstances that police had originally raised about Candace. She had wondered what kind of parents would raise a daughter who would run away—just like police had wondered about her and Cliff.

Wilma suddenly had a new appreciation for the pressures and challenges facing police. She had seen the world through their eyes.

....

Camp Arnes was working towards a computerized system which included entering the names of all their campers into a database. Wilma had volunteered to help in the process, knowing that getting back into a work routine was good for her.

It was early in the spring when she was alphabetically weeding her way through the large stack of cards, finally coming to those whose last names began with the letter D.

And there it was.

CANDACE WYNNE DERKSEN,
BIRTHDAY JULY 6, 1971,
WINNIPEG, MANITOBA.

Wilma was frozen. Part of her job was to eliminate cards that were no longer current. She took a closer look at Candace's card, which included a spot for counsellor comments.

"Candace was a great girl, her attitude was superb," one Camp Arnes employee had written.

"Spiritually, I could see that she took her faith very seriously," a second worker had noted.

"Strong Christian. She interacts well with her peer group, and she does her work well and with enthusiasm. She has lots of knowledge about the Bible and participated. She was helpful. She hardly mentioned the fact that her parents were at camp," a third counsellor had stated.

Wilma smiled. She was proud of her daughter for not trying to use Cliff's role as the summer program director to curry favour with the staff. She had been trying to find her own way at the camp, just as she was doing in life.

Wilma didn't know what to do with the card. She grabbed another piece of paper and copied down every word, tucking the finished product in her pocket. She then took the original camp card in her trembling hands, struggling to keep her pencil steady as she updated her daughter's status and placed it back in the file.

"DECEASED."

14

Adjusting. I think that is what they call one of the stages of grief where, whether you want to or not, you realize that you have to continue to live, so you do. Every minute, every second of every day, we were reminded of Candace. Every time I laid out five plates instead of four, I had to put that fifth plate back into the cupboard. And every time I returned that plate, I knew that in a tiny way I was cutting more of Candace out of our lives. I had never realized before how much a part of our lives she was, how much a part of our subconscious, until we tried to live without her. It was like amputating my right arm without any anaesthetic. I think it was doubly difficult because this was the time when we wanted to preserve her memory; we wanted to keep part of her alive forever. And yet we found that in order to function normally, we were removing her little by little from our lives. It seemed so unfair.

....

Odia Derksen was flipping through the pages of a comic book when she abruptly put it down and turned to her mother. There was clearly something on her mind.

"This wouldn't have happened, Mom, if you had picked Candace up when she called," she said.

The words cut sharply through Wilma. It was the first time her 10-year-old had ever expressed anything resembling anger about the circumstances of that fateful day. Wilma wasn't sure how to respond. Odia was now standing, seemingly ready to leave the room.

"Odia, sit here and let's talk about this," Wilma said. She could sense her daughter's discomfort. Wilma ached for her.

"You're right. I should have picked Candace up. Odia, if I could redo that day, I would pick her up. I'd sit outside that school all day just to make sure I didn't miss her. She was that important to us," Wilma said. "When there is a tragedy like this, we look for someone to blame. And the easiest thing to do is to take all of the blame, bundle it up, and lay it on one person—usually the person closest to us. But we can't do that. When something happens, there are usually a lot of people that are at fault. I should have picked her up. The police should have listened to us. Dad should have come home earlier that day. But none of us wanted to hurt Candace. I didn't tie Candace up and leave her in a shack to die. Most of the blame has to land on the person who actually did it. Candace should have been able to walk home from school safely."

Odia stared at the floor the entire time. The adjustment to life without Candace was clearly bothering her more than Wilma had imagined.

"Next time you feel angry with me for not picking Candace up, remember that I'm sorry too. It's the one regret that I have to live with the rest of my life," Wilma continued. "And Odia, we'll never let this happen again."

....

Wilma knew there would be many more difficult family conversations in the weeks, months and years ahead. Syras would eventually start asking questions about his big sister. Wilma vowed to always be open and honest with her children. She wanted them to feel safe and comfortable sharing whatever was on their minds.

Odia seemed to be relishing the opportunity to speak candidly about Candace. She came home from school one day, clearly upset by something that had happened. It only took a bit of prodding to reveal that several kids had been making a series of awful jokes on the playground.

"It's a stupid joke. The joke is: What did the Derksens get for Christmas? Candy in a box," said Odia.

Wilma couldn't believe how cruel some kids could be.

"Odia, there are always going to be people around who enjoy hurting other people. Someone very cruel hurt Candace," Wilma said. "Candace was hurt, and we are being hurt, too. We have to be kind to everyone, even those who hurt us. But I also want you to be careful around people who like to hurt others. You can't take them seriously."

....

Had Candace Derksen's killer struck again? Winnipeg police certainly thought that might be the case. Only this time the victim had somehow survived.

Just months after Candace's body was found, a 12-year-old girl was discovered tied up and screaming inside an empty railway car on Gateway Avenue. A woman who happened to walking in the area heard the girl's cries for help and came to her rescue. She found a clearly distraught Patricia Wilson sitting upright in the boxcar, in the process of loosening the rope around her wrists. A plastic bag was loosely placed around her head.

"Mommy, Mommy," Patricia was yelling.

The girl was a student at Valley Gardens junior high school, living with her parents in East Kildonan just a few miles away from where Candace Derksen lived.

That wasn't the only thing. Patricia told police she had been grabbed off the street earlier that afternoon, shortly after she began walking home from school. She claimed her attacker was a man but didn't get a good look at him. She said he brought her to the railcar, tied her up and then fled the scene. She reported no other assault, either physical or sexual. Police noted the reported abduction happened around 4 p.m. on a Friday—exactly the same as Candace.

There was more. A package of chewing gum was found inside the boxcar. Gum had also been left behind in the shed where Candace's body was found. Police wondered if this was a coincidence or a criminal calling card. It was yet another mysterious development that had police investigators puzzled.

....

The ground had been broken. And plans were well under way for construction of the Candace Derksen Memorial Pool at Camp Arnes. At first, it had seemed like an impossible dream. Total cost of the enclosed pool was estimated at $250,000. But the outpouring of community support had made it a reality.

Numerous suppliers had pledged donations of materials and resources to work on construction. The Manitoba government had donated $30,000, nearly matching the total raised by the grassroots community fundraising campaign. It was a remarkable effort that overwhelmed the Derksens.

Family, friends and a large network of supporters gathered at the construction site on a glorious late summer day to officially dedicate the start of the project, which included a large swimming pool with diving board, a Jacuzzi whirlpool, a sauna and change rooms. Construction was expected to take one year.

Harold Jantz, a close Derksen family friend, welcomed everyone to the event with a moving speech.

"There is one word that came to my mind when I thought of this occasion. It was 'remember'. We have come to this place this afternoon to remember Candace Derksen and to dedicate a memorial to her memory. She will be remembered by the swimming pool which is to be erected at this place. We will remember the many emotions that she stirred in so many of us as we lived through the events of last winter, her disappearance, the weeks of uncertainty, the endless agony of doubt about what she might be experiencing until at last the largest question was answered.

"We will never forget the prayers and hope which surrounded her parents, Cliff and Wilma, and Odia and Syras. We stood with them and yet in a sense we didn't. There were some things that only they as a family could carry. We remember how well they carried them and how deeply their faith and forgiving spirit moved not only us but a whole city.

"If this memorial is to signify anything at all, it should be a reminder for us to remember some very important things. They reminded us of the importance of family and good times experienced within the family. They could talk about the good times they had swimming together. The family that swims together, stays together. They shared with us in very simple ways how they talked about Christian faith and the hope that believers have that they will someday be able to enjoy heaven together in the presence of God.

"For Candace in her childlike way, heaven included a swimming pool.

"They reminded us that a loving relationship with God can prepare people to face even the most agonizing experiences in life. Without making extravagant claims for themselves, they demonstrated to us that evil can be met with good, that love is stronger than hate.

"Together with others, they taught us the importance of even one life. They helped us to cherish a child for the promise of that life and showed us how important it is when a child has parents and community who can surround it in times of trouble and grief, who will rally to them when danger threatens. They helped us to think of other lost children when it was one child we were concerned about.

"None of us who were close to the Derksens during this time will ever be the same again. And I want to encourage us all to remember some of the lessons we learned. It is this that helps give meaning to her death, and in small ways we begin to see how God can bring good out of tragedy and evil.

"People who have placed their faith in a good God, who can believe that He is there even in the midst of tragedy and evil, who can forgive when the natural response might be to lash out with bitterness and revenge, can also experience the wonder of restoration and healing. The Derksens are a witness to that truth.

"In the final analysis, that is what this dedication here today is all about. That is why we remember. Not so that we might wish for retribution, but so that we could hope that restoration might continue. So that good could continue to result."

....

SATURDAY, NOVEMBER 30, 1985

The anniversary day fell on a Saturday, and when we got up that morning it had all the markings of being just an ordinary day. I wondered if by ignoring it, just not talking about it, we might not really notice it.

But right from the beginning, even without any words, I could tell that a cloud had descended on us. Even the kids sensed it and seemed preoccupied.

By afternoon I was desperate to escape from the heavy mood, and I tried to arouse Cliff into making some last-minute plans. Couldn't we at least go shopping?

Cliff had retreated to the basement to work on the computer, and he looked up from the swirl of papers, irritated. I suddenly knew that his absorption was his escape, and he was comfortable in it.

I prowled around the house a bit longer and then decided that maybe Cliff had the right idea. I needed to drown myself in work, in hard work. The hardest work I could think of was washing walls.

I should have known it wouldn't work. I'm never in the best of moods when I'm housecleaning as it is; why would it be any different this day of all days? I could tell that instead of losing myself in the scrubbing, I was just becoming more and more irritated.

I stared at the hundreds and hundreds of little fingerprints. Did the kids touch the walls all the time? Were they blind? Did they find it impossible to walk down a hall or down the stairs without feeling where they were going?

As I worked my way down the stairwell, I glanced at my watch. It was getting closer and closer to four o'clock. I started to understand the importance of an anniversary. It is probably the closest to the original moment one ever gets.

Time seemed to stand still. Why was this moment so terrifying? What actually happened this time a year ago? Suddenly I knew! This was not only the anniversary of the day that Candace disappeared; it was also the anniversary of my decision not to pick her up.

There were fingerprints on the wall above the bottom step, and I wondered how they had gotten there. Cliff and I never touched that section of wall, and Odia and Syras were too small. Only Candace, like every teen I knew, would hang onto the doorjamb and swing herself out over the main floor. I looked closer. They were her size. They were Candace's fingerprints!

Immobilized, I sat on the stairs looking up at them. I couldn't wash them off. So little of her was left. How could I remove more evidence of her life?

Without looking at my watch, I knew what time it was. It was five minutes after four. The moment was heavy with expectation, as if Candace might call any minute and I would be able to get into the car and pick her up and save all of us from going through the year of pain. We would have Candace again.

The wishful moment didn't last long. Suddenly the expectations turned into accusations. Why hadn't I picked her up?

This time there was no answer.

What kind of mother would allow her daughter to walk home in the cold at such a vulnerable time? Why hadn't I foreseen what was going to happen? There had been a number of other times when I had sensed that my children were in danger. I had found them perched precariously on top of the stairs or in the kitchen with a knife, but I had always been there to prevent the accident.

This time, when the danger had been the most hostile, I had been preoccupied with cleaning the downstairs.

Why hadn't we been able to convince the police to get out the dogs when the scent was fresh? We had done nothing! While she froze to death in a shed, we had been sitting in a warm house just waiting for her to die.

It was all my fault. I could have prevented all of it from happening. She had died, and I had the audacity to survive and go on living.

The fingerprints seemed to grow larger.

PART TWO

15

He shuffled slowly down a Main Street sidewalk, paying little attention to morning rush-hour traffic. It was time for another day at the office. He expected today would be a lot less eventful than yesterday. After all, there weren't going to be any national television crews coming to interview him about his rather tedious work of picking up garbage off the streets.

And that was perfectly fine for a man who preferred to simply blend into the background. Nothing about his life was glamorous, although there was some satisfaction in knowing his efforts were being noticed.

He was just a few blocks away from reaching Siloam Mission when several men suddenly came out of nowhere and surrounded him.

"Mark Grant?" they said to him, a serious look on their faces.

He nodded his head in agreement. They took another step closer.

"You're under arrest for the murder of Candace Derksen."

....

Cliff and Wilma Derksen received the call early in the morning. Now, just a few hours later, they were seated at the head podium of a jam-packed Winnipeg police news conference. The news has spread quickly around town, thanks largely to the recent surge in social media. The Derksen family barely had time to digest what had happened before meeting the media.

"We are stunned the case has come to this point," Cliff said.

"It just feels like our lives have been turned upside down again," Wilma added.

There were no overt public celebrations, no proclamations of justice finally being served. Reporters asked the typical questions—Did they ever think this day would come? Was there now a feeling of closure? How had they survived the past 22 and a half years?

Cliff and Wilma spoke eloquently about being sustained by their faith, the closeness of family and enduring friendships. They acknowledged the hard part might still be before them as the case wound through the courts, which were unpredictable.

"The story is not finished," Wilma said. "It's just started."

Winnipeg police Insp. Tom Legge was seated at the same podium, providing a general overview about how they'd broken open one of Winnipeg's most notorious unsolved mysteries. Police were being careful not to give too much away, knowing anything they say could ultimately be used against them once the case got to court.

Legge credited the hard work of the cold case unit, praising the efforts of Sgt. Al Bradbury, Const. Jon Lutz and others. He shared the fact the suspect, Mark Grant, had been interviewed by police during the initial investigation but offered no other details. He said Grant only recently became a "person of interest" but didn't specifically say why.

Winnipeg police Chief Jack Ewatski, one of the original investigators on the case, also declined to provide further details. They had come this far that nobody wanted to risk giving a defence lawyer ammunition to use against them.

Police spoke vaguely of DNA evidence but held back specifics. Legge confirmed that police had used a piece of Grant's discarded gum to test against DNA profiles that had been created from the original evidence.

"This one was obviously a match for us," Legge said.

Several police sources would begin filling in a few blanks later in the day, telling reporters about the renewed forensic investigation.

"We called it Project Angel after Candace," one officer said privately. "She was just an innocent kid, a good kid."

....

Alison Bartel had spent more than two decades wondering who killed her good friend. Now, like many Manitoba residents, she was stunned by news of an arrest.

"It was a life-changing thing, for the school, for everybody who knew her, for the city ... there's nobody who doesn't remember it," Bartel told the *Winnipeg Free Press* just hours after learning police had seemingly solved the murder mystery.

Bartel was one of Candace's schoolmates at Mennonite Brethren Collegiate Institute, and took horse-back-riding lessons with the 13-year-old on weekends. She recalled being let out of class to search for her friend and how Candace's disappearance disturbed the entire community. Parents forbade their children from walking alone and children were frightened to go anywhere.

"It was horribly scary," she said. "I don't think I slept the same for weeks, months, and nobody went to or from anywhere alone. You were afraid to go to school, you were afraid to walk to the corner store."

Dave Loewen, who helped lead the civilian search committee for Candace, was still reeling when contacted by reporters. He recalled how schoolmates of Candace distributed orange flyers publicizing her disappearance in the 12 square blocks between her Talbot Avenue school and her Herbert Avenue home.

"The co-operation from all sectors of society was outstanding," said Loewen. "There was a lot of compassion and support for this. It was such a bizarre disappearance. There was a lot of support, but no clues ... we went door-to-door in that whole area and inquired everywhere. I'll tell you why, and we talked about that right away, the hardest thing is not to know. When her body was found, then we knew what had happened, and where she was, and that was very consoling. We couldn't imagine having to live without knowing she was dead or alive ... of course, the preference would have been to find her alive and in good shape. But, the worst would have been not to know."

Loewen revealed how he'd spoken with police in February and had a feeling they might be closing in on a suspect.

"It never left us ... the police were so sincere about trying to resolve it," he said,

Dave Teigrob, vice-principal at Candace's school in 1985, told reporters how all those who knew Candace were profoundly affected by her death. He continued working at MBCI until 1994 and was now living in Saskatchewan.

"It had a huge impact on the school and on the students. People didn't have a sense anything like that could happen," said Teigrob. "That (Grade 7) class was profoundly affected. Right through the entire lifetime of their movement through the school, it was always like there was a concern, there was an empty chair where Candace should've been, even through to graduation."

....

They had no idea a suspected killer was in their midst. Staff at Siloam Mission was as stunned as anyone to learn the truth about one of the newest recruits to their Mission: Off the Street Team employment training program.

John Mohan, executive director of Siloam, said they had no idea about Mark Grant's criminal past or the fact he had been the subject of a community sexual offender notification in December 2005 because of his high risk of sexual violence.

"We were surprised that he was on a warning list for suspected predators. Our hearts are overwhelmed for the

Derksen family, and our thoughts and prayers are with them at this time," Mohan said in a statement.

Siloam Mission chief operating officer Garth Reesor said Grant had been referred to the MOST program by Winnipeg's Forensic Psychological Services, a sex offender treatment program, about three weeks ago. He said Siloam accepted Grant because in the past Grant had had a difficult time holding down a job. Reesor said during his time with the program, Grant posed no problems.

"He worked as part of the team," he said. "He was not active in anything else at Siloam."

Grant's appearance had changed since the 2005 notification. He had lost about 30 lbs. and his hair was almost white. He had been living in a basement apartment on Sherbrook Street in Winnipeg's core area. Neighbours said he was quiet and kept to himself.

Amazingly, the popular Christian television program *100 Huntley Street* had just interviewed Grant a day earlier as part of a documentary they were preparing on the MOST program. Officials said the interview would never be broadcast now that Grant was a suspect in murder case.

Siloam staff only learned about Grant's arrest when he didn't show up for work. Hours later, officials with forensic psychological services called them with the news. As a result, the Princess Street shelter was now exploring the possibility of doing criminal background checks on people entrusted to jobs or programs.

"Safety is paramount at Siloam," said Reesor.

16

The date had always loomed large on the calendar, filling them with a sense of dread and overwhelming sadness. But the Derksen family usually spent November 30th the same way every year—struggling to sort through a myriad of emotions that always seemed to become more vivid on this particular day.

The 20th anniversary—November 30, 2004—proved to be more challenging than most. Several local media outlets were doing "where are they now" stories and began contacting the family for advance interviews. Looking back, the date marked a turning point in the investigation.

Cliff and Wilma had been as accommodating as ever, believing every written or broadcast word about Candace was a tribute to her memory and another opportunity to get the answers they so desperately sought. The couple explained to reporters how a typical year was now filled with a variety of highs and lows.

"We've never made November 30th a special day— we keep it low-key. But her birthday is a time of joy—it's a victory and it's a party. July 6th we have fun," Wilma told the *Winnipeg Free Press* at the time. "On November 30th, we do something sad. And January 17th, the day they found Candace, is another sad one."

"We've tried every possible way of getting through it," Cliff added. "We've tried ignoring it, going to church, everything."

The Derksens repeated their long-held belief that someday justice would finally be served. They credited the ongoing support of family and friends, neighbours and strangers who had helped them get through the darkest days of their lives and remain strong.

"The memories are still there—it just doesn't seem like it has been 20 years," said Cliff. "The memories are hard, but we've come to accept that. We've put it behind us for now. But if they find the perpetrator it will be a new chapter we'll face."

Unfortunately, the high-profile nature of Candace's case also brought out some of the worst in society. Cliff and Wilma were still stunned by the two people who had phoned their home years earlier to confess.

"It was just sick," Cliff said. "Especially with the first one, I thought it was legit. I was in trauma because I couldn't believe I was talking with the person who did this to my daughter. Once police investigated them and found they were pranks, I thought it was just unbelievably cruel."

Cliff and Wilma had spent countless hours over the years thinking about what Candace might have become had she not been stolen from them. Their consensus— Candace would have certainly graduated from high school, but likely would have balked at pursuing her post-secondary education. She always enjoyed the social aspect of school but had trouble staying focused on the work. Candace likely would have found her calling working with children, perhaps at a daycare centre. She most certainly would have become a mother. They would have grandchildren by now.

"She would have married someone. She'd be in a nice house, with nice clothes," Wilma told reporters. "She was a party person, but not in a negative way. She was a much more social person. She had a social gift. She put on parties for everyone. She could have been an event planner."

As always, Wilma was forced to address the issue that continued to haunt her.

"I still regret not picking Candace up when she phoned for a ride," Wilma said in that 2004 interview. "The other decisions we made we can live with. There's guilt. It's just one of those things where you're left with guilt. But it has also been a driving force for me."

Cliff had been down this road many times before. He reached out to Wilma, wrapping a comforting arm around her.

"You make decisions in life—it didn't seem that big of a decision at the time," Cliff said quickly.

....

Winnipeg police had also made themselves available for interviews around the time of the 20th anniversary. But it's what they didn't say that would prove to be most revealing. Publicly, investigators stressed one key message—they weren't giving up. Privately, a no-holds-barred investigation was about to get underway that would prove to be their final shot at catching Candace's killer.

During the interviews, police dropped a few subtle hints. They noted there had been major advances made in the field of forensic sciences over the past few years. This provided new hope, however faint, that Candace's killer would one day be caught.

Police also reminded the public they still held several strands of hair found inside the shed with Candace's body. They hoped this would ultimately prove to be the proverbial smoking gun, thanks to the rapidly advancing science of DNA identification.

It was now widely accepted that DNA is a genetic fingerprint. No two people have the same DNA. Blood, saliva, hair and semen all contain DNA and have been routinely collected at crime scenes since the mid-1990s. DNA profiles from convicted offenders are now submitted to the National DNA Data Bank in Ottawa, which is run by the RCMP. DNA profiles taken from crime scenes in cases in which there have been no arrests are also submitted in the hope that a match will be made.

Sgt. Al Bradbury and Det. Scot Halley of the Winnipeg Police Service's cold case homicide unit had just been assigned as lead investigators on the case. Bradbury joined the police service in 1987 but felt a strong attachment to the case. He told media in 2004 that even the most seemingly insignificant information could be helpful.

"They may think it's minimal information, but it could be huge for us," he said. "A homicide never goes away. Just because time goes by doesn't mean you get to take a walk."

Police said publicly they had followed up a couple of theories—that Candace was stalked by a sexual predator or was a victim of a prank gone wrong—but neither connected her death to a specific suspect. They had been deluged with tips. Every one was followed up and catalogued by teams of officers assigned to the case. What was learned in this case is now the template for how similar investigations are managed.

"The public response was huge," retired Winnipeg police Staff Insp. George Pike said in a 2004 interview with the *Winnipeg Free Press* in anticipation of the 20th anniversary. "This was a very senseless act. There was no logic behind it."

Pike and police Chief Jack Ewatski were continuing to vow that Candace's killer would be identified. Ewatski was a sergeant in what was then the robbery-homicide squad at the time Candace's body was found while Pike led the detectives working on the investigation.

Ewatski told the *Free Press* the shed in which Candace was found was still sealed in a police evidence warehouse near Polo Park Shopping Centre. He said the shed—its four walls, roof and floor folded up—was in police hands because of the forensic evidence it contained. Investigators suspected the assailant had a manipulative personality and may have had interests in bizarre subjects, like bondage. The person also likely lived in the area and knew about the shed. At the time of Candace's death, DNA analysis for law-enforcement purposes was in its infancy. However, because of the circumstances of Candace's death, investigators made a decision to keep the shed in the possibility it could someday reveal her killer.

There was other reason for optimism. Winnipeg police had used DNA to arrest three men in connection with the October 24, 1987, slaying of Erwin Kakoschke in Winnipeg. The suspects were arrested in 2001 after DNA analysis was done on two cigarette butts found at Kakoschke's Norris Road house. Kakoschke, 63, did not smoke.

Police believed in 2004 that Candace's killer had left behind similar forensic clues for them. It was just a matter of time, patience and diligence before they cracked them.

....

The years had eroded much of the anger Cliff and Wilma Derksen had about the police response in those initial days. They now had a better understanding, if not acceptance, of why officers didn't immediately act with a sense of urgency upon the initial missing persons report being filed.

There were so many initial theories. Maybe Candace had just carelessly run off to a friend's house and forgot about calling home. Could she have been mad at her Wilma for not picking her up? Did she just run away to blow off some steam? Cliff and Wilma had always known this was nonsense. They no longer faulted police for not realizing this as quickly as they did. How could anyone have predicted the awful truth of that day?

"Police follow procedures, and initially they, not knowing who we were, missed a window of opportunity,"

Cliff said in a 2004 interview with the *Free Press*. "I'm not faulting them, but that's the way it is. We figure the only way it will be solved is by accident."

"There was a window to catch the person, but after this long now it has to be by chance," added Wilma. "We just assumed they'd get out there right away, but they didn't."

Cliff and Wilma continued to take solace in knowing their daughter was not sexually assaulted—although they still believed that was the initial intention.

"The reason why he didn't go through with raping her, we'll never know," Cliff said. "Police did say they spent some time there. It's possible he realized she was innocent and didn't go through with it."

Police had speculated Candace may have spent several hours with her killer.

"They talked. There were conversations. We give Candace credit that maybe she talked him out of what he was planning to do," said Cliff. "The guy might have left, but if she was terrified she might have stayed there waiting and then it was too late. Maybe she thought she could wait for morning. She would think in the shed she was safe. She might have been too young to appreciate the danger of a cold Winnipeg night."

Cliff still had a difficult time accepting the fact police once considered him a possible suspect in his daughter's disappearance. He believed some of the initial focus on him proved to be a missed opportunity for police.

"I felt at first, well, they have to go through the routine, but it was frustrating because they were putting their energy there instead of elsewhere," he said. Although he passed his lie detector test and removed any doubts, Cliff believed the focus on him helped cause the killer's trail to go cold.

With all the time that had passed, Cliff and Wilma openly questioned in 2004 what news of an arrest would do to them. In many ways, they feared the whirlwind of publicity and odyssey through the legal system that would surely follow.

"I don't relish going through it. It wouldn't be pleasant, but we'd do it," said Cliff.

"If they're dangerous, we want them dealt with," Wilma quickly added. She said it was also possible that the killer was deceased. "Maybe there's nobody carrying this secret out there," she said.

The couple's strong Mennonite faith has helped sustain them all these years. But Cliff and Wilma admitted their faith caused people to misunderstand them.

"Our desire to forgive was misunderstood by a lot of people at the time," Cliff said in 2004. "Some people thought we didn't want to have the perpetrator to ever be charged. The forgiveness we expressed was for our own personal survival."

Odia was just nine at the time her older sister vanished. She was now married and taking fine arts. One of her recent projects, called *Last Walk*, was a booklet about her sister complete with quotes from her mother's book on the disappearance overlaid over black and white photos showing the route Candace would have taken to get home that day.

Candace's brother, Syras, was only three at the time she went missing. His memories of Candace are mostly from the family photographs and reminisces. "To him, she was somebody who babysat him and as a friend," Cliff said. Syras was now entering the field of psychology. Cliff and Wilma wondered whether, in some way, his sister's death and the way his parents dealt with it helped determine his career choice.

Life had also continued for Heidi Harms, now Friesen, Candace's best friend who showed up for a sleepover the night of November 30th, 1984 only to be greeted by the frantic search. Two decades later, Friesen had been married for 11 years, had four children aged three to nine and was living in the United States while her husband completed his PhD.

"Countless times, I've thought she should be there," Friesen told the *Free Press* in late 2004. "She should have been part of my wedding. It's a feeling of not knowing who should be the first to call with both good news and bad news. I've never been able to develop a friendship like that with anyone else."

Friesen said Candace's disappearance was something she thought about frequently, especially near the anniversary date and at night. "Twenty years later and it still comes up in my dreams," said Friesen. "In my dreams, I'm always searching and can't find her."

Wilma and Cliff have gone through many stages as they dealt with their loss through the years. "At 10 years, we both hit a wall," said Wilma. "I think we ran out of anger and energy. It was a surprise because we thought at the seven-year mark we were coming out of it. Then we went into a wilderness."

Wilma spoke openly about her desire to affect change in Candace's memory by working with the Mennonite Central Committee on programs designed to help victims of crime. She had released a book on her daughter's case, called *Have You Seen Candace?* which chronicled the family's tragic loss.

Wilma had also taken on the role of director of Victims' Voice, a national program to assist families affected by homicide and violent crime, and also Victim Companions, which offers support and volunteer companions to crime victims, and Safe Justice Encounters, which helps victims deal with issues by meeting with offenders. The family was also proud of their work in helping the fledgling Child Find grow in Winnipeg as one of the country's strongest chapters. The Derksens had 20 years of experience as victims under the belts. At this point, they told reporters in 2004, they were ready for whatever life threw at them.

"When you get to this time, you're going through the past and the what-ifs. What if I'd have taken another job or something—would this have happened? We made decisions, like which way to go with issues of her passing, the grief, the forgiveness—did we make the right decisions? I think we made all the right ones," Cliff said.

"Our lives haven't been perfect, but we haven't been destroyed," Wilma added.

As Candace's landmark anniversary passed, the family would once again fade from the headlines. And police were quietly about to take Project Angel to the next level.

17

The public was learning a lot about Candace's alleged killer, thanks to National Parole Board documents that quickly became the talk of the town.

"Mark Grant is a schizophrenic whose mind is filled with disturbing rape fantasies, lust for vulnerable teens, a hatred of women and an unwillingness to take any treatment for his perversions," according to one of many decisions the federal agency had delivered against Grant over the years.

The documents painted a chilling picture of Grant's extensive criminal history and attitude towards his victims. Grant had spent nearly 13 years in prison from 1991 to 2004—save for a nine-day stretch of parole when he raped another young woman. Behind bars, Grant alluded to other sex crimes dating as far back as the 1970s for which he was never charged. Yet he never disclosed specific details nor mentioned Candace Derksen. Justice officials had grave concern for the safety of any young woman who had contact with him.

"Your sexual/assaultive behaviour has resulted in serious harm to the victims. You have been predatory in your choice of victims, often looking for unsophisticated and vulnerable post-pubescent female children," the parole board wrote in revoking his parole in 1995. "The board is satisfied that, if released, you are likely to commit an offence causing the death of or serious harm to another person before the expiration of your sentence."

It noted Grant's self-reported "sexually deviant" behaviour that hadn't resulted in criminal charges—including raping a drunk female stranger. He linked his "hatred of women" to the behaviour of his mother and sister and being "victimized" as a child but gave no specifics. He also refused any type of treatment—such as chemical castration—that would have reduced his sexual urges.

"You are considered to be more concerned about your own sexual gratification than you are about the consequences your offending causes to others," the parole board wrote in 2004. "You admit your sexual gratification comes from the vulnerability of young women and children as 'they are so trusting.'"

Testing of Grant revealed an "elevated level of arousal to rape stimuli" with the highest peaks occurring "with material depicting inappropriate sexual contacts with children, predominantly to female."

Mark Grant had escaped from jail and was wanted on a Canada-wide warrant at the time he allegedly kidnapped and murdered Candace Derksen. His criminal record at the time included a prior assault conviction against an underage sex trade worker, plus convictions for forgery, fraud, break and enter, escape and failing to comply with court orders.

Grant had been in custody since May 24, 1984 following an arrest for break and enter, but escaped from an unspecified facility on November 7th that year. He was 21 years old at the time Candace was grabbed off the street.

Grant was arrested on December 7th on the outstanding warrant, then quizzed by police on December 10th about any knowledge he may have had regarding Candace's disappearance. Police were especially curious because a teen they claimed was Grant's girlfriend at the time, 15-year-old Audrey Manulak, said Candace had been "hanging around" with them in the previous weeks.

"Grant indicated that he had no knowledge of Derksen other than what he had learned from the media," Const. Jon Lutz wrote in the police affidavit.

Grant admitted during his December interview with police to dyeing his hair red shortly after escaping from jail. Police eventually recovered an empty box of light blond hair colouring from near Grant's home. The hair-dye revelation was a key reason Grant continued to be a person of interest for Winnipeg police, according to the court documents. Grant also admitted dyeing the hair of Manulak, whose story raised all kinds of suspicion for police.

"She was found to be untruthful in a number of matters regarding the missing person investigation and most of what she related could not be relied on," wrote Lutz.

Still, they had no evidence. And the trail would go cold for many, many years. The Derksen case would gather dust for the next six years, although Grant remained a potential suspect. He was convicted of three sex assaults between 1989 and 1994 that ultimately resulted in prison terms of more than 13 years.

In November 1991 he was convicted of raping a young woman and given four years in prison. In July 1994 he was released on parole, then brutally raped a 22-year-old sex trade worker nine days later. She told court Grant approached her downtown and invited her for a beer at his place nearby. She went, and he locked the deadbolt as soon they got inside.

"And then I turned around and he grabbed my throat and pushed me on the couch," she said. Grant pulled her hair and moved her into the bedroom, ordered her to stick out her tongue and then tried to bite it off before raping her. "He told me I better not go see any cops or he'd kill me," she said. She picked Grant out of a photo line-up. His parole was revoked and he was eventually sentenced to nine years in prison.

"I consider Mr. Grant to be the worst offender and the facts of this case to be the worst set of facts," said Queen's Bench Justice Perry Schulman at the time. The new time was added to the existing sentence, meaning his parole was re-calculated and the full sentence wouldn't expire until September 2004. Grant served every minute of the sentence, as parole was denied based on his continuing rejection of treatment and what the board deemed an "enormous" risk of re-offending.

He was released at the end of his sentence but sub-jected to a peace bond application by Winnipeg police and a public alert through the Community Notification Advisory Committee. Conditions included staying away from children. The order expired in late 2005, and police issued a second warning to the community.

"Information recently received about Grant has raised concern that his risk to re-offend has increased significantly. All adult females and children (both male and female) are at risk of sexual violence," police said in a release.

It was around this time that police officers began taking another look at Grant as a potential suspect in Candace Derksen's abduction and killing.

....

Three pubic hairs were found on or near Candace's body, while four scalp hairs that appeared to have been lightly bleached near the roots were on her clothing. Police weren't able to test the seven hair strands for DNA until July 1993, after the technology had improved but by that time police were on a different investigative path and looking at a dangerous sex offender as a potential suspect.

Stanley Pomfret had just been arrested and charged with killing a Winnipeg teen and raping and torturing two others. Police sent the seized hair exhibits from the Derksen crime scene to the RCMP forensic lab for comparison to Pomfret's hair. The RCMP lab replied that two scalp hairs "had significant similarities" to Pomfret's hair. However, there was an insufficient quantity and quality of hair to produce a usable DNA profile, the court document said. The hairs weren't compared to any other potential suspects, including Grant, at the time.

Police tried another form of DNA testing in 1995, this time sending the RCMP a piece of gum seized from the Derksen crime scene. Although male DNA was found, no profile could be obtained. They took another crack at DNA testing in 2001. They resubmitted the seven hair samples and chewing gum for testing but again met with frustration—no known profiles were obtained.

In 2007, just days after the arrest of Mark Grant, Winnipeg police spoke out against the national RCMP lab for what they called outdated technology and restrictive policies. Investigators suggested they may have been able to crack the cold case more than five years earlier if Ottawa's National DNA Data Bank had been better equipped.

"The exhibits were returned to us. There was either an inability or an incapability to proceed further in examining the exhibits," Insp. Tom Legge explained. "From a policeman's point of view we need that lab to do up-to-date work for us."

He called on federal politicians to make sure the lab got the funding it needed to bring it up to speed with dozens of privately run labs in Canada and the United States.

"It's a tool we use more often than the public realizes," Legge said of DNA analysis to solve crimes. His comments echoed those made by federal Auditor General Sheila Fraser in a scathing review of the National DNA Data Bank. Fraser said the RCMP-run lab was beset by backlogs and "significant weaknesses" in how it dealt with quality issues, particularly with an automated process for testing DNA.

Legge revealed some additional details about the investigation, saying police had a small pool of suspects and wanted the RCMP lab in Ottawa to analyze forensic evidence recovered in the shed to see if it came from the same person. If so, that DNA profile could be tested against known offenders who had been ordered by the courts to supply a blood sample for DNA purposes.

But, Legge said, the federal lab did not have adequate technology. He said officers eventually learned of Molecular World Inc., a private lab in Thunder Bay that had the ability to run more extensive hair-shaft DNA tests than the Mounties offered. The testing involved identifying the "maternal lineage" of the subject donor, which is DNA passed from mother to child

Dr. Amarjit Chahal, general manager and laboratory director of Molecular World Inc., told reporters how they'd used DNA analysis to solve one of the most notorious American murder cases.

Scott Peterson was convicted of the sensational killing of his wife Laci and their unborn son in 2002 in San Francisco. The science of testing hair for a DNA profile gained prominence in Peterson's murder trial when a single strand of Laci's hair was used to help convict her husband of the slaying. In Canada, the science was less known, but was accepted by an Ontario court for the first time in 2006 in the conviction of Ronald Woodcock for murdering two men and trying to kill four others.

"The technology is now being accepted this side of the border," Chahal told the *Winnipeg Free Press*.

Chahal said Molecular World was the only approved lab in Canada that specialized in testing hair for a DNA profile—called mitochondrial DNA. DNA from body fluids is nuclear DNA. In the Peterson case, prosecutors used a one-inch strand of hair found in a pair of pliers on the boat Peterson took fishing the day his pregnant wife disappeared, which matched the genetic code of Laci and her mother. That hair helped the prosecution show Peterson used the boat to move his wife on the day she vanished Christmas Eve 2002. Her remains were found that April.

Unfortunately, Winnipeg police could not send the Thunder Bay DNA profile of the suspect to the national DNA lab for comparison, nor could it ask the national lab to borrow a known offender's blood DNA sample, as the federal lab had policies of not sharing material with private labs. Legge said that meant police had to obtain new DNA samples from their suspect and have Molecular World compare them to what was recovered in the shed in 1985.

Hence the beginning of "Project Angel's" attempts to secretly seize the needed exhibits from Mark Grant.

....

Police tracked Grant down in December 2006 and reinterviewed him about the Derksen case. He had been released from prison in 2004 and was the subject of two separate public warnings that he continued to pose a high risk of sexually reoffending.

"Grant denied knowing the deceased or having any involvement in the homicide. Grant was asked to provide a voluntary DNA sample and refused to do so," Const. Lutz wrote in the affidavit.

Police decided to put Grant under surveillance and obtain his DNA for comparison to DNA in the seven hair strands from the Derksen crime scene that they sent to the Ontario lab. There was also testing to be done on a piece of rope found around the young victim.

Several fresh samples were obtained from Grant earlier that year without his knowledge. Police found some of his scalp and pubic hairs sitting in an evidence-control storage facility that dated back to his first sexual assault arrest in 1989. They lucked upon a blood sample of Grant's after he was shot inside a Spence Street rooming house in March 2007. He suffered a leg wound. Police seized his bloody pants as evidence and sent three swabs to Ontario. They began following Grant on a regular basis and obtained a saliva sample when they saw him spit on a sidewalk just a few weeks before his arrest. They rushed in to scoop it up moments later.

The Ontario lab got back to police in April with the results: The hair samples and rope offered a match with Grant's DNA. Police finally had the killer in their sights.

18

They found a comfortable table near the back of the darkened lounge and settled in for what they expected was going to be a long evening. A local journalist had arranged the meeting at the posh downtown Winnipeg hotel. He wanted to take them on a trip down memory lane. In many ways, it all seemed so surreal.

Yet here they were, two of Candace Derksen's closest friends, seated at the same table reflecting on the awful day she went missing, the immediate aftermath and how their lives had moved on in the nearly 23 years that had passed. They had lived, they had loved—but they had never forgotten what they had lost.

. . . .

David Wiebe still remembers the snowball fight like it was yesterday. The school day was over and Wiebe, then 15, slipped up to Candace with an icy surprise in his hands. She never saw it coming.

"Candace was on the phone, in the basement of the school, and I threw the snow in her face," Wiebe told the reporter with a mischievous smile.

A stunned Candace had started giggling.

"She was talking to her mom, who asked what happened. She said 'David just threw snow in my face'," he said.

Wiebe later caught Candace in the school parking lot and threw some more snow at her. She wasn't about to complain. Wiebe knew he was her major league "crush."

Wiebe had eyes for Candace, too. Only he wouldn't have dared tell her. Their age difference was one thing. But another issue entirely was the fact they were actually four grades apart. Wiebe had skipped a grade, while Candace had been held back a year.

"Candace was attractive in every way. She was so vibrant, so full of life. She was just a great, great girl," Wiebe told the reporter.

His tone changed as he recalled asking Candace where she was headed. He remembered offering to walk her home, but that he had Drivers Ed and had to stay at school.

It was later that evening when Wiebe spoke with Wilma Derksen for the first time. She had come to the school where he was at choir practice and quickly introduced herself.

"Do you know where Candace is?" she asked, a sense of urgency in her voice.

Wiebe told her he'd watched Candace leave school hours earlier, headed home.

"She never came home," Wilma replied.

"I'm sure she'll show up," said David.

But she wouldn't. Not that night. Not ever.

....

Heidi Friesen had been looking forward to a great visit with her best friend. She and Candace were inseparable, especially in summers when Candace and her family would spend several weeks out at Camp Arnes, which Heidi's family ran. They had had big plans for this visit. There would be gossiping, singing, laughing and, of course, talking about boys like David Wiebe.

"We were so boy-crazy back then," Friesen recalled.

Her father dropped her off early that morning, and Friesen rushed to the front door of the Derksen house, expecting Candace to greet her with a hug. The door was slightly ajar. Wilma answered her knock, looking worried.

"Candace is missing," she said.

A nervous Friesen went over to her sister's home, where police showed up a few hours later to talk to her. They were clearly thinking Candace had run away. Friesen's father interjected. "If you think she's a runaway, then you don't know the family," he told officers.

David Wiebe recalled how he would also get a visit from police in the coming days. He remembered being home with his parents when a burly officer showed up at the door and said he needed to speak to their 15-year-old son alone. His parents remained downstairs while Wiebe and the officer spoke in an upstairs bedroom. He remembers thinking the officer was bringing good news. It was anything but.

"I'm going to have Candace back in my office by midnight tonight," the officer began. Then he dropped the anvil. "You know why? Because you're going to tell me where she is."

Wiebe was stunned. He remembers bursting into tears, repeatedly denying he had any knowledge about Candace.

The officer didn't seem to believe him. Later that evening, Wiebe went to a movie with one of his friends. He recalls being followed to the theatre by a police cruiser car.

"I couldn't believe it," he told the reporter.

....

Heidi Friesen had been at her school in the Interlake the day Candace's body was found on January 17th, 1985. Other students heard about it during lunch and made a pact not to tell Friesen, knowing how hard she would take it.

"I was dropped off on the bus that day, got home and walked inside. My dad was crying. He said 'Candace is dead'." Friesen couldn't, wouldn't believe it. "No, no she's not dead. She's not dead," she said.

David Wiebe was in choir when the Mennonite Brethren principal walked in. "I regret to inform you Candace Derksen body has been found," he said.

Wiebe slumped against a wall, "bawling his eyes out," while a classmate put a comforting hand on his shoulder.

Friesen said she'd clung to the hope Candace was alive, although she always feared something awful had happened. "I thought she'd been abducted and forced to work as a prostitute," she said.

Wiebe said he cried himself to sleep for many nights, listening to the song "Friends" by Michael W. Smith. The Christian singer was loved by Candace, who often quoted his lyrics in her letters to Friesen.

Friesen still cherishes her memories and mementos of time spent with Candace through a variety of ways, including photos of them together, diary entries and even the sweatshirt Candace wore for her school picture.

Candace went missing just days before the school pictures came back. The photo was given to police and media outlets, and has become an image frozen in the minds of many.

....

Wiebe and Friesen had remained close with Cliff and Wilma Derksen all these years. They had always held out hope that one day her killer would be caught.

"I basically shut myself off from friends, just withdrew for a while. I didn't want to get close to anyone again," said Wiebe.

"I lost my childhood. I had to grow up fast," added Friesen, whose mother had died of cancer when she was seven.

The past caught up with the present for Wiebe on Valentine's Day, 2007. Winnipeg police wanted to speak with him about Candace. It was an almost unbearable case of déjà vu. The murder investigation was making progress and police said they wanted to take all necessary steps to eliminate Wiebe as a suspect. Again.

He was told everything was voluntary and he could leave at any time. Despite his feeling of dread, Wiebe said he'd do anything he could to help. "I figured if I was the Derksens, I'd be grateful if everyone did everything they could," he said.

So he rolled up his sleeves and gave a blood sample, answered police questions on videotape and let himself be hooked up for a polygraph test. Wiebe hadn't prepared himself, though, for the onslaught of questions from the stone-faced investigators.

"Did you kill Candace? Do you know who killed Candace? Why'd you kill Candace?"

Wiebe said he felt the tears coming on, just as they had nearly 23 years earlier when the big police officer interrogated him in his bedroom while his parents sat downstairs.

"You might as well have stuck a knife in my heart," he said. "I was just thinking, why do I have to go through this again?"

Wiebe passed the test and the police told him they wouldn't call again. Although he hoped that was true, he had doubts. He wondered whether police were actually making progress or simply taking another shot in the dark.

....

News of Mark Grant's arrest had left them speechless.

Friesen said it should send a chill up the spines of others who thought they'd gotten away with the perfect crime.

"This DNA stuff works. Your time is coming," she said.

Friesen is now happily married and a mother of four kids. Wiebe and his wife have two young ones. Both admit to being especially protective. And both say they look at Cliff and Wilma Derksen as inspirations.

"They're just wonderful people. They've overcome such tremendous obstacles," said Wiebe.

Friesen said she felt "a sense of peace" since she learned of the arrest and hoped that wouldn't be shattered by the looming justice process, which could take a big toll on participants. "I can't imagine going through this without the community of faith that we have," she said.

Wiebe said he would someday like to speak with Candace's killer to ask one simple question.

Why?

"Candace did nothing wrong. Nothing," he said.

19

There were hundreds of pages of documents, each one forming another piece of the puzzle that was Mark Grant. His contact with the justice system had been extensive, the expert reports on what "made him tick" numerous.

Grant's initial criminal history was fairly routine. He pleaded guilty in February 1983 to false pretenses and uttering a forged document and was given probation. In September 1983, he pleaded guilty to assault causing bodily harm and breaching probation, receiving six months of custody.

Grant was back before the courts in November 1983 on theft charges, for which he was given a $100 fine. Another arrest followed in December 1983 for possession of marijuana. He was given a conditional discharge.

He admitted to credit card fraud in July 1984, receiving three months. At this point, he was already facing new charges of break, enter and theft for which he was to remain in custody. But Grant escaped from jail on November 7th, 1984 while on a medical escort and remained at large until one week after Candace Derksen vanished.

He pleaded guilty to the break-and-enter and escape custody charges in March 1985 and was given two years behind bars. In February 1986, Grant admitted to assaulting a police officer and received two months. He pleaded guilty to passing more bad cheques in October 1987 and got 18 months probation. In March 1988, Grant was charged with possession of stolen goods and was given a two years suspended sentence.

Then came the start of his sexual offending. In May 1988 he admitted to the sexual assault of a teenaged girl and was given 30 months in prison. He pleaded guilty in December 1989 to another sexual assault of a young woman and was given four years. Finally, he was convicted of sexual assault and choking to overcome resistance in August 1994 and got nine years, for which he would serve every last day.

....

Dr. Richard Howes wrote the first detailed report on Grant's background in November 1994, shortly after his return to Stony Mountain. A clinical psychologist at the federal prison, he was blunt in his assessment of Grant.

> It has been suggested Mr. Grant's sexual offences might be explained as a function of chronic anger at his inadequate upbringing, and this is a perfectly reasonable explanation. What I would add to this, however, is a greater emphasis on the component of rejection in his childhood and early adulthood, for in my view he is uniquely vulnerable to any perception of rejection. In spite of some earlier reports that Mr. Grant attempted to explain his first sexual assault of a 16-year-old acquaintance as simply the product of her fear of her parents reaction to a consenting sexual

relationship, he specifically acknowledged to me that it had indeed been an offence of rape because the victim (although originally consenting during foreplay according to him) clearly resisted him at one point and he proceeded to force himself on her in spite of this. He could not, in short, accept her rejection of him. In a parallel manner his second sexual offence appears to have been motivated by anger at rejection by a friend, who allegedly exploited the friendship and even revealed indifference to a gesture of self-mutilation by Mr. Grant. Mr Grant then punished this friend by raping the friend's girlfriend.

That Mr Grant is an intensely troubled individual cannot reasonably be at issue with his multiple suicidal attempts or at least gestures giving stark testimony to this. The unhappy circumstances of the abuse, neglect and indifference he experienced in his childhood also exacted a significant toll, and his assertion that "my family despises me" suggests that there has been no improvement on this dimension. A component of conditioned self-loathing may also be present, and in explanation of his general criminal history Mr. Grant suggests that in a sense he has been punishing himself because he is not worthy of freedom. Problems in relationships have been at the forefront of his dysfunctional living pattern, and he recognizes that he moves too quickly in his desperate search for love and acceptance. As an example he reports that he was out of jail for only nine

days before he commenced a common-law relationship (with a woman who had corresponded with him
while he was incarcerated) and they were making
plans for a formal marriage and talking about starting a family. Aside from the haste with which he
was moving, it might also be argued that his choice
of romantic partners has not typically been very dis-
criminating (although in candour he hardly repre-
sented a prize catch himself by virtue of his criminal
irresponsibility and emotional instability).

Attending briefly to psychological tests, Mr.
Grant is similar to the profiles of individuals com-
monly described as introverted, impulsive, mistrustful, anxious about the future and moderately
depressed. His score on a measure of intelligence fell
in the low average range, which suggests that he is
capable of benefitting from upgrading beyond his
reported grade six academic level.

In response to my query about why he believed
detention was unnecessary in his case, Mr. Grant
argued that he has the treatment resources in place
to reduce his risk and he believes that he has some
employment prospects or might return to school. In
describing what he has learned thus far from his treatment program participation, he avows that he recognizes keeping anger in was a problem and that he
now expresses his anger through his poetry and distracting himself with general reading until he is better
prepared to deal with a particular problem. He also

reports having learned that he must improve his education in order to improve his employment prospects.

Mr. Grant cannot offer any explanation as to
why he sought out a prostitute (the victim in his most
recent offence) when he was in a new common-law
relationship, and too many times Mr. Grant simply
responded "I never thought about that" in answer to
my questions for me to develop any confidence that he
is fully aware of his offence cycle. While he describes
many of his actions as "stupid", his general level of
insight does not appear to me to be very profound.

All in all I do not have great confidence Mr.
Grant will suddenly embrace a conventional, responsible lifestyle following his release, although whether or not any irresponsibility will be translated into
violent offending is clearly impossible to predict with
any reasonable measure of clinical certainty.

. . . .

Janine Cutler, a well-known psychologist who works with
sexual offenders, was next to take a shot at getting inside
Grant's head. She authored a report in 1995 while Grant
was being considered as a candidate for a federal mental
health program.

Mr. Grant was pleasant and co-operative throughout
the assessment process. He presents as being quite
anxious and depressed. He is still adjusting to being
back in prison, and is unsure of his placement status. These facts account for some of his anxious and
depressed state. Mr. Grant presents as being very

needy and states he needs and wants therapy. Mr. Grant considers himself to be emotionally unstable. He has had psychiatric difficulties in the past.

Both the interview process and psychological testing indicated that Mr. Grant is a very anxious, depressed, angry and emotionally injured individual. He is consumed with feelings of hopelessness, morbid thoughts and a preoccupation with death. Emotionally, Mr. Grant has great difficulty with both emotion and affection. Interpersonally, he is not attached to any-one. He has problems with relationships in general, and in particular with women. Mr. Grant is a very angry individual, and he could act out his anger in a very primitive, uncontrolled manner. He is capable of acting out violently, both towards himself (suicidal tendencies) and towards others. Mr. Grant has bound-ary issues and, therefore, often is not able to separate himself from his environment. He also uses denial as a major defence mechanism. Cognitively, Mr. Grant experiences paranoia, confused thinking and lapses in reality testing. His primitive anger, boundary issues, poor reality testing and general suspiciousness of oth-ers suggests that Mr. Grant may be dangerous, in that he could easily act out violently.

....

Grant ultimately was moved to a regional psychiatric cen-tre for specialized treatment of his sexual offending.

Dorothy Reid, the program supervisor, completed a detailed report of Grant's progress. Grant was hoping the completion of the program might pave the way for him to be released on parole at some point prior to serving his full nine-year sentence.

Mr. Grant had three disclosure groups. The first focused on his history, offences and the abuses he was subjected to as a child. He was able to share both the sexual and physical abuse inflicted upon him by his parents and siblings. His willingness to disclose marked a positive approach to understanding his behaviour. The second group outlined his crime cycle. Here Mr. Grant was able to outline some of his past behaviour and the impact it had upon the build up and the acting out phases of his crime cycle. Mr. Grant was encouraged not to spend most of the day in bed and a more active role in his environment. As a start, Mr. Grant agreed with the feedback from the group and committed himself to go off the unit and interact with others. He did this for a brief period and returned to his usual behaviour and as a result he has gained a substantial amount of weight in the abdominal region. Mr. Grant is fully aware of the things he should be doing but does not display much enthusiasm and drive. When approached he acknowledges his shortcomings but does little to change his behaviour. Mr. Grant was able to prepare a relapse prevention plan and identifies his risk factors which include: not taking anti psychotic medications, owning and possessing pornographic magazines, harbouring fantasies of a sadistic nature, being in a dysfunctional relationship, loneliness and refusing to communicate his feelings with others.

Mr. Grant revealed that on previous incarceration he did not empathize with his victims and as a result disregarded the rights of others. Through the teaching sessions, he was able to define the concept of empathy and provide some examples outside his own personal experience.

Mr. Grant recognizes that his values and beliefs were distorted. He can now identify his negative thoughts and feelings more readily and is learning to change his negative thinking by challenging his thoughts. In so doing, Mr Grant is able to see how his actions led to his offending behaviour. At present, he is better to check his behaviour and as a result make more appropriate choices.

Throughout the program, Mr. Grant has been generally pleasant with the demands placed on him by the treatment team but does not take much pride in his external appearance.

His present discharge plan includes staying in a halfway house for a six month period prior to release to Winnipeg. He is in contact with a woman whom he met while she was visit his parent institution as a church volunteer. Mr. Grant anticipates starting a common-law relationship with her upon release.

The variables affecting Mr. Grant's risk to re-offend relate to a juvenile history of deviant sexual behaviour and at least three other offences. Those offences occurred when he was not taking medications. He was diagnosed with schizophrenia from an early age and since then has been treated with antipsychotics and an anti-depressant. He also has a history of suicide attempts.

The dynamic factors influencing his potential risk to re-offend hinges on his ability to utilize the skills he has learned. On a positive side Mr. Grant is able to express himself in a more assertive manner and initiate social interaction with other patients. However, his willingness to remain on medication remains a concern. While at his parent institution, Mr. Grant abstained from taking his anti-psychotic medication on several occasions with the view of experiencing increased sexual stimulation (one of the side effects of his medication is an inability to achieve an erection). He has acknowledged that within two days of ceasing his medication, he begins to experience violent sexual fantasies. During the presentation of his crime cycle, it was stressed that Mr. Grant must continue taking his medications daily.

While Mr Grant expresses the desire to return to the community, he is not highly motivated to live a productive lifestyle. He also sees incarceration as a more appealing alternative to living in society.

. . . .

Wilma Derksen sat down at her kitchen table, flipped open her laptop computer and began typing. She had decided to call her new blog "Lemonade", a perfect testament to the resilience she had always preached as a victim.

"When life hands you lemons, make lemonade" were good words to live by, and Wilma thought they perfectly captured the essence of the thoughts she planned to share with readers now that her daughter's killer had seemingly been caught.

Writing had always been therapeutic for Wilma, which is what prompted her to sit down in the late 1980s and begin putting her deepest thoughts on paper. The end result was *Have You Seen Candace,* Wilma's intensely personal look at the first year following her daughter's disappearance. The book was published in 1991 and Wilma relished the opportunity to tell the story, especially knowing how much it would assist other families in similar tragic circumstances.

A second book, called *Confronting the Horror: The Aftermath of Violence*, was published in 2002 to serve as a roadmap for other victims of crime and document the various stages of grief she endured.

Wilma spent three years volunteering with the new Child Find Chapter in Winnipeg before beginning work with another new organization, called Family Survivors of Homicide.

In 1996, she began directing a Victims' Voice Program through Mennonite Central Committee's Canadian office in Winnipeg. It was yet another opportunity to help others.

Through it all, Wilma continued to write. Now, she was embracing the opportunity to reach even more people that had been presented by the virtual, online world. Her first blog entry had come surprisingly easy. But that wouldn't always be the case.

> *I'm watching my husband mold a head for his clay sculpture, a couple dancing. I have an office down the hall where I could work, but I'd rather sit here next to him and share his messy table because there is simply nothing more enjoyable than watching an artist intent on his work. I'll even endure the play-by-play commentary of a football game on the radio he's listening to.*
>
> *He holds the head up, examines it and chuckles. I could describe this head that he is fashioning out of clay to you and you might smile too, but I won't— not here. It is his to unveil.*
>
> *He starts on the second head—that of a woman, a clump of unshapely clay which will become another cartoon character within a half hour, like magic, emerging out of nowhere. I'm envious, as a writer it takes me fifty pages to create a well-rounded character that he can produce in minutes, a picture is worth a thousand words, and I can see it happening as she becomes an instant fictional character. I shouldn't give the impression that all of it is easy. There have been times when I thought he was done with a piece, but then he folds it into a ball again to try again— a truly resilient potter.*
>
> *This reminds me of our theme on this website which is to explore resilience and the crime victim.*

I'm not choosing this theme because I feel particularly resilient at this time in my life. I continue to struggle with every issue, every event, and in my creativity, every word. None of it is easy. And I'm not choosing it because I feel I am an expert on resilience. I first noticed the word this year.

However, I do know that when I see pictures of resilience, hear stories of resilience or meet people who exude resilience, I'm inspired. The word carries with it a surge of empowerment and inspiration.

When we workshopped resilience over a six week period last winter, it generated a good group discussion. Over the years I have participated in many focus groups on many subjects, such as trauma, forgiveness, justice, victims' needs, restorative justice—but nothing has been as enjoyable. In fact it was exhilarating.

I also know that I need to be resilient now. Our daughter was murdered 23 years ago, and it is only now that someone has been charged with her murder. We have no idea what this will mean in our future.

After spending about twenty years focused on the darkness, the horror of crime, I am in the mood for something light, something new, something optimistic—but still meaningful and powerful.

It's one o'clock in the morning. My husband has finished fastening his two heads onto the dancing figures and we laugh. It is such a comical sculpture—he turns it around, and we laugh again.

20

Mark Grant's paperwork continued to pile up during his time behind bars. And it was now providing a revealing look into the makeup of a man police believed was a cold-blooded killer.

Dr. Richard Howes completed another risk assessment in early 2000, once again with a view towards a possible parole bid by Grant. His findings quickly shot down any hopes Grant had for an early exit and would pave the way for parole rejections in 2001, 2002, 2003 and 2004.

By his own admission Mr. Grant recognizes that his history of sexual assaults was motivated by his passionate, entrenched anger against people in general and women in particular. This chronic anger clearly originated in his tumultuous background where he was a victim of serious, protracted physical, sexual and emotional abuse. Functional abandonment by his natural mother, abuse and ridicule by his stepmother, neglect by his reportedly alcoholic father, and sexual molestation and further ridicule by his stepsiblings were all a part of a childhood and adolescence which led naturally to his pattern of harming both himself and others. Mr. Grant reports that he grew up hating both women and men, and he uses words such as "revenge" and expressions such as "trying to get even" to explain himself. He has frequently engaged in self-mutilation. I submit his anger at women is so profound he can probably still rationalize his assaults. In other words the sense of personal moral outrage at their offending which exerts a strong controlling effect for many offenders does not likely exist in Mr. Grant. He can certainly articulate an understanding of concepts such as victim empathy, but this appears more intellectual than heartfelt. His risk of reoffending is substantially elevated by this weakness.

According to Mr. Grant none of his sexual offences have been committed while he was either drunk or high—an assertion which I know of no evidence to contradict, and thus we cannot find reassurance in the possibility that his risk will be diminished if he remains abstinent. He reports having used drugs such as LSD and cocaine, but he maintains that only his use of pot has been excessive over the years. He does not view this marijuana use as a risk factor, for he maintains that it actually mellows him and his anger does not emerge when he is using. He may be quite right about this, but the unfortunate conclusion must be that his risk of reoffending remains significant because he was fully aware of his actions and not simply disinhibited by a toxic influence he might learn to control.

Of particular relevance in considering Mr. Grant's risk of violent reoffending is his mental status.

He has been diagnosed as schizophrenic and is currently on medication to control his symptoms. He reports that when he quits taking his medication he becomes depressed, edgy, paranoid and suicidal.

Among these high risk factors would be included: major mental illness with command hallucinations (currently in remission, but only while he is compliant with prescribed drug treatment); the strong likelihood that he will again fail to comply with his prescribed treatment, especially when he knows that doing so will restore his sexual arousal; emotional instability, which in an important way is distinct from his major mental illness; the presence of chronic anger, especially at women, arising from a tragically abusive background; significant doubts about whether he is capable of developing meaningful victim empathy; his recent treatment termination by two therapists for a lack of progress and commitment; the early onset of his criminality; his multiple previous sexual offences (not all of which came to the attention of authorities); the gratuitous violence displayed during his offences; his reoffending while on previous statutory releases; his failed treatment program participating as evidenced by sexual reoffending.

In short, I am unequivocal in concluding that Mr. Grant represents a high risk to reoffend violently and thus his detention is warranted. If he is serious about making choices to reduces his risk and properly prepare himself for a return to the community then he will strive to use the remains of his sentence more profitably than he has thus far.

At the moment, however, Mr. Grant represents an unacceptably high risk of continuing his established pattern of sexual offending and the interests of the community will best be served by detaining him.

....

Grant didn't handle the negative report well, as another review in late 2000 proved.

Mr. Grant has continued to reside at the mental health range at Stony Mountain. Grant was placed on suicide observation from Sept. 24 to his release on Sept 26. Grant had self requested this placement as he had been feeling depressed over a lengthy period of time and felt that he was losing control of his ability to keep himself safe. The case management team feels that his ongoing use of marijuana within the institution is also a factor in his decompensation. Currently Mr. Grant relates that he has not used such substances in over six weeks but still struggles with a desire to use.

Grant was shipped out of province to yet another specialized sex offender program in July 2001. Yet a 2002 report on his so-called progress continued to be mostly negative.

The offender was diagnosed with paranoid schizophrenia and depressive episodes at age 12. He has tried many antipsychotics in the past. Grant has a history of suicide attempts, which are triggered by anxiety, paranoia, or dysphoric moods. He reports that he has attempted suicide approximately 20 times by hanging, slashing and overdose. He states that he has slashed to release tension and feelings of worthlessness.

During the admission period he continued to have intermittent auditory hallucinations. He had increased paranoid ideation and some generalized anxiety. He felt that it would be bothersome to people if he told them how he was feeling. He reported experiencing auditory hallucinations but stated he was able to cope with them by using self talk. The hallucinations tell him to harm himself, that he is no good, and that he doesn't deserve to live. He denied any self-harming intent at that time.

Grant maintained a low profile on the unit. He attended group and school consistently and progressed well in both. He felt he deserved to feel depressed due to past behaviour. However he was able to manage his depression and denied any feelings of self hate. He socialized appropriately, approached staff with requests and concerns and was not a management problem.

The offender has identified the following personal warning signs of relapse, and has defined the severity levels of each. He expressed an understanding of the dangers of taking illicit drugs and using alcohol; however, he often talked and joked about drinking upon release. He said "I have come to realize and come to see that drugs and alcohol have no place in my life and I have come a long way."

The offender has accepted and dealt with his diagnosis of diabetes on Jan 21, 2002 in a responsible manner. He tests his blood sugar levels regularly and takes his diabetic medication as prescribed. He is struggling with the diabetic diet but is open to teaching.

Grant's last institutional offence was 4.5 years ago, Nov 19, 1997. From March 1993 to that date he had incurred 7 serious charges and 4 minor charges. He had 2 convictions for fighting and 4 convictions for substance use, 1 conviction for being verbally abusive to staff. The 4 remaining charges were for disobeying rules.

On April 22, 2001, the offender superficially slashed his arm and reported it to staff. He was taken to healthcare. He stated that he had done this to release frustration. He had phoned his father in the morning. His father was still drunk, talking down to him and abusing him at the same time. He informed that his father drinks everyday and all the time. Issues with his father had been building up. He promised no further self-harm.

Grant realizes that his lifestyle contributed to his offending behaviour. He understands that his behaviour was influenced by his substance use, unwillingness to deal with his mental illness, generalized anger and his negative attitude towards women. He does not wish to live this lifestyle, or return to prison. He accepts responsibility for his crimes. The offender recognizes that he will need structure, support and supervision on release into the community. He wishes release to a halfway house, so that he can integrate slowly into the community. He is desirous of programs and counselling.

Grant reported that his sexual fantasies were of consenting sexual relations with age-appropriate women. He denied experiencing fantasies of non-consensual sex, or of sex with age inappropriate partners. However, in the past Grant has reported fantasies of violent and non-consenting sexual relations. Moreover, his offences all involved violence (slapping, dragging, choking and threatening victims). On inquiry, Grant indicated that he is quite open about the types of partners that interest him. This is consistent with his working as a prostitute as a young man, and with the wide range of ages of his victims.

Grant began masturbating to violent fantasies in order to soothe feelings of anger and distress at the young age of eight. He currently reports only occasional use of sexual fantasies or masturbation to soothe upset or angry feelings, claiming that he habitually uses distraction instead. He continues to view sexual activity as essential to his well being and is unwilling to interfere with it. The nature of his offences and prior self report both suggest that a strong and deviant sex drive has been present and has contributed to sexual offending in the past.

When asked about his offending behaviour, Grant was not able to give a detailed or comprehensive account of what leads him to offend. Therefore I base my analysis on file information and elements of Grant's self report. When this account was presented to him, Grant agreed that it described his offence pattern.

It appears that Grant's offence pattern begins with an urgent desire for intimacy and sexual gratification. He stops his medication in anticipation of sexual activity. However, he also feels certain that those he desires will reject him. He tries to cope with this by increasing his use of substances and by establishing a relationship with a woman who is interested in him, but whom he does not see as particularly attractive. He struggles with deep feelings of hostility and anger at the woman he is involved with and those he believes would reject him if he approached them. His behaviour towards his partner then becomes increasingly hostile and abusive, he sooths his painful feelings by masturbating to violent fantasies, pornography, fantasies of women he sees in public, or by hiring prostitutes. Within a fairly short time, his anger and hatred reach the point where he finds a vulnerable victim and violently sexually assaults her, thus regaining a sense of mastery and domination through the control of his victim.

....

Grant returned to Stony Mountain from the federal sex offender program in 2002—now less than two years away from his full sentence expiring—and continued to raise red flags.

A late 2002 progress report revealed major concerns.

> It was reported to staff on separate occasions in July 2002 that Grant was cheeking his medication and giving it to another offender. He was defiant and defensive. He informed that he goes off his medication occasionally in order to masturbate. Also, he stated that he traded the drugs for tobacco. It is apparent he is not internalizing what he is learning. The unwillingness to give up self-defeating behaviours indicates that he is unwilling to manage his risk.

Another damning report on Grant came in December 2002 from officials with Stony Mountain.

> It is the opinion of the writer that Mr. Grant has not been up front and honest about the majority of his life and offending history. He presents as a changed individual by his ability to verbalize his knowledge. However, these changes are not reflected in his everyday actions and behaviours. As well, Mr. Grant is overly reliant on the amount of programming he has taken while incarcerated and feels that he should be judged solely on this. In conclusion, Mr. Grant has completed the sex offender treatment program. Although he has a good knowledge base and some awareness about his pattern of offending, he has not

internalized these changes to the point of mitigating his risk to sexually reoffend.

Mr. Grant recalled a history of family abuse and violence while growing up. He reports that he did not have any friends because the acquaintances he met were not able to frequent his home. He reports that they were sent away by his parents. Mr. Grant reported feelings of normalcy as a result of the regular physical and sexual abuse from his siblings. He stated that he felt some satisfaction knowing that he had been fulfilling others' desires, and he stated that this was the reason for his behaviour on the street.

Mr. Grant stated he felt he could not have a normal relationship due to his low self-esteem and this he stated was the reason for his frequenting of hookers.

Mr. Grant's attitude toward women was noted as critical. He did not express any respect for women and suggested that they would use anything they could to demean men. Perhaps this was reflective of the lifestyle he possessed while growing up.

....

"People usually consider walking on water or in thin air a miracle. But I think the real miracle is not to walk either on water or thin air, but to walk on earth. Every day we are engaged in a miracle which we don't even recognize; a blue sky, white clouds, green leaves, the black curious eyes of a child—our own two eyes. All is a miracle."
—THICH NHAT HANGH

Would you meet with him?

People ask me that question a lot these days … usually after a pause signalling to me the gravity of this place in the conversation.

'I don't know,' I answer … and in all honesty I really don't know. I've been asked this question for the last 24 years even when no one was charged. The question is not about the accused. At this point we still don't really know who is guilty. The question is whether we would meet with the person who killed our daughter? I don't know.

Actually I don't know a lot of things these days. I don't know why I stopped writing on this wonderful website a few months ago. I had such lofty intentions to tell these wonderful stories and have my husband draw these cute cartoons to explore resilience. It was fun getting going, and everyone pitched in … and then I stopped. I felt suddenly like hiding. I get like that sometimes. I'm an introvert and I prefer to process things in private. Or it could have been a simple writer's block. I don't know.

When I'm in this reclusive mood, I want to spin back the time and be hippies again. For both Cliff and I, the hippy era conjures up memories of a time in life when we traveled across Canada, young children and all, following our bliss. We were creative back then. No one saw any of it—but we could decorate houses, wear whatever we wanted, paint huge pictures, and write crazy poems with abandon. We believed the world was ours. And it was…

Then we began to take life seriously, and life became very serious—way too serious. Now we yearn to recover that flush of first love of life to be free, to create, and to retreat.

So here I am in my garden—my hippy garden—where everything just happens on its own. We created this secret garden to be intentionally slightly chaotic, a bit wild. But now even in its naturalness there is a sacred harmony to it, a harmony that comes when the plants are left to grow into their place. I trust this sacred harmony, and I have come to the garden to be reminded of that power.

But I know that I can't run away from life, just as I can't run away from the question. Would you meet with him? I know that the question isn't about "meeting" anyone really, the question is about life, and laden with layers and layers of all of life's issues, conflicts, pain, woundedness, fear, anger, hazards and possibilities.

Right now, at least for me, the bigger question is what do you do if you are stuck and need to process? Apparently you don't have to write a book anymore—you blog through it.

Now that is terrifying … And I don't know if I can do this.

21

Preparations were underway for Mark Grant's preliminary hearing, in which a provincial court judge would
decide if there was sufficient evidence to move the case
to trial. Grant remained in custody, having briefly flirt-
ed with the idea of making a bail application about six
months after his arrest. He filed an affidavit, through
his lawyer, outlining a proposed bail plan which included going back to work for Siloam Mission by cleaning
downtown streets at $8 per hour.

Grant also floated the idea of having three long-time
friends post at least $10,000 in sureties, and promised to
continue seeing psychiatrists and psychologists three times
per week while also undergoing drug and alcohol testing.
He claimed a woman he had known for 20 years—whom
he described as his common-law wife—who was seriously
ill and about to undergo open heart surgery.

A date was set for a bail hearing, yet ultimately
abandoned by Grant. No reasons were provided to the
court. Crown and defence lawyers were continuing to
review mountains of evidence and documents related to
the prosecution.

One of the more interesting revelations was a January
2006 letter written from Grant's treating psychologist

to Winnipeg police and the high-risk offender unit of Manitoba justice. Janine Cutler disclosed in the letter how Grant's time back in the community following his September 2004 release from prison had initially gone smoothly. But she discussed several major concerns which had prompted officials to issue a rare second public alert about Grant in December 2005.

Cutler's lengthy letter began by outlining a troubling relationship Grant had developed shortly after getting out of jail, while living under the terms of his initial year-long peace bond.

> I am writing this letter in response to your request for a brief summary outlining the significant developments that warranted my contacting the Winnipeg Police Services high risk offender unit, the risk factors that led to such concern, and my opinion regarding Mr Grant's current risk and possible risk management in the community.
>
> I initially met Mr. Grant when I worked at Stony Mountain Institute, first as the psychologist associated with the mental health program and the mental health range and then as the senior psychologist.
>
> Over time a growing concern developed in regard to his relationship with a man he interacted with on an ongoing basis, for a variety of reasons. First, it very quickly became readily apparent to all members of Mr. Grant's team that this man was a very negative influence in his life, as he appeared to be attempting to work at cross purposes with

Mr. Grant's treatment, support and case management team and convince Mr. Grant to abstain from using the services he was receiving.

Second, Mr. Grant began to take on a very protective role with his friend's wife, and his relationship with her appeared to be changing in nature over time. Based upon the information provided by Mr. Grant, it appeared that she also liked to consume alcohol and did so in his presence. Finally, although Mr. Grant's probation officer instructed both Mr. Grant and his friend that Mr. Grant was not to be at his friend's home when his granddaughter was present, subsequent to finding out this couple had their granddaughter living with them, his friend continued to bring Mr. Grant to his home when his granddaughter was present.

Cutler said that officials with Child and Family Services were contacted to speak directly to the family, warning them that any further contact with Grant would likely result in the child being seized.

Cutler said Grant expressed concern about the fact his initial one-year order had expired in September 2005. Her letter continued:

Mr. Grant reported engaging in alcohol usage after his peace bond ended as a way of celebrating the occasion. As Mr. Grant continued to see his friend and his wife on a regular basis and, according to Mr. Grant they consumed alcohol at least socially, I noted that this was an area that needed to be monitored.

In addition, Mr. Grant's attendance at the recreational evening program had begun to wane, and he was now spending a greater amount of time in the evenings with friends at their home. Needless to say, this caused concern.

During Mr. Grant's psychotherapy/sex offender treatment on Dec. 1, 2005, he informed me that he had quit school the day before. Mr. Grant also reported that he had not been attending school very much because he was spending a fair amount of time during the day with his friend's wife, with whom he was in love. Mr. Grant previously had stated that his friend was abusive and controlling in his relationship and that he would never let his wife leave him. Over the course of the session, Mr. Grant spoke about his relationship with the friend's wife at length.

Although Mr. Grant's treatment, support and risk management team previously had considered Mr. Grant's relationship with this couple to be an unhealthy and destabilizing one, his increased involvement with his friend's wife and time spent at their home was alarming.

Cutler said Grant then dropped another bombshell:

He informed me that he had been going to the bus stop every morning to see a woman, that is, that he had been stalking her. During the discussion he also revealed that he had been experiencing rape fantasies about her.

Mr. Grant and I devised a plan whereby he would meet with me the following morning, and every morning the next week, at 7:30 a.m., so that he would not attend the bus stop at 8 a.m. and I could help him break the cycle in which he appeared to be entrenched.

Grant revealed he had been watching the woman for approximately three straight months in late 2005, yet had never approached her or considered acting on his fantasies. Still, there was grave concern expressed by Cutler— which only intensified when Grant failed to show up for their meeting the following morning.

Grant claimed he was too tired due to his medications and would make it the following day. Once again, he was a no-show. This prompted Cutler to contact Winnipeg police and pen her letter.

Currently Mr. Grant is residing in the community in an unstructured and unsupervised environment without the benefit of appropriate treatment and support. Without medication, it is highly likely that Mr. Grant is experiencing psychiatric symptomatology, including auditory command hallucinations. As a result of his propensity for violence and sexual offending, self reported rape fantasies and stalking behaviour, probable substance abuse and psychiatric instability, Mr. Grant is at extremely high risk for re-offending.

Justice officials were quickly able to obtain a new one-year peace bond against Grant in December 2005, based on the concerns raised by Cutler. Police also vowed to keep an even closer watch over him.

Of course, that wouldn't be difficult since he was about to become the prime suspect in Candace Derksen's killing and would be under frequent surveillance until he was finally arrested in May 2007.

....

THURSDAY SEPTEMBER 10, 2009

"It was wonderful to go back in time and feel Candace again. It was as if she was in the courtroom with us."

Wilma Derksen stood outside the downtown Winnipeg courthouse, feeling a sense of relief mixed with nervous anticipation. Moments earlier, provincial court Judge Tim Preston had wrapped up a three-week preliminary hearing by ordering Mark Grant to stand trial for first-degree murder. The outcome was hardly surprising, given that there is a much lower standard of proof required at a prelim than what a judge and jury face at a trial.

The Crown had presented a slimmed-down version of their case, calling only the evidence they felt was necessary to establish there was at least some evidence which could prove the charge against Grant.

Defence lawyer Saul Simmonds had done the same, offering up very little challenge to what was presented in court. Like all good defence lawyers, Simmonds wasn't about to tip his hand and reveal potential defence strategies in what was essentially a legal dress rehearsal. He planned to save it for the big stage, where both the Crown's burden of proof and the stakes would be much higher.

A court-ordered ban meant only the outcome of the hearing could be revealed. The public would have to wait a while to hear the full scope of the case police and prosecutors had built against Grant.

The Derksens were warned that a trial could still be years away, considering it was expected to be a lengthy and potentially heated affair filled with all kinds of legal twists and turns. Like always, the family was simply taking each development in stride.

"We just think it's a huge gift to even be having this process," Wilma told the media. "After so many years, we'd given up."

PART THREE

22

It was one of the most gripping murder mysteries in Winnipeg's history. So it was inevitable that finding 12 unbiased citizens to sit on a jury and weigh the evidence was going to be a difficult task.

The case had touched so many people over the years. And now that it was time for it to finally go to trial, justice officials were concerned the passage of time had done little to close the wounds of a fragile community.

On a cold winter day—not unlike the day Candace Derksen vanished—about 170 Winnipeg residents appeared at the downtown Law Courts unaware of the enormous challenge that was waiting for them. None of randomly selected potential jurors had been told ahead of time the notorious murder mystery they may be ordered to preside over.

Crown and defence lawyers had made certain agreements in advance of jury selection. Those included being able to screen potential jurors for any prior knowledge and/or opinions they may have about the case and the man about to go on trial. The move—called "challenging for cause"—is common in high-profile cases in which there are fears the publicity surrounding the case could potentially poison the jury pool.

Queen's Bench Justice Glenn Joyal, who would be presiding over the upcoming trial, had pre-approved a list of four questions lawyers would be allowed to ask. They included whether the potential juror had heard of Candace Derksen's death, knew anything about Mark Grant and whether the person felt they could be impartial.

The lawyers would be assisted by two civilians who were sworn in as jury judges. They would not actually sit on the jury but would help lawyers decide whether the prospective jurors being screened appeared to be biased. If no reason was found to dismiss them from performing their civic duty, the onus would fall on the Crown and defence lawyers to choose whether they wished to accept or reject the juror.

By law, each lawyer could reject up to 20 jurors without giving any cause. Perhaps they didn't like the way certain questions were answered. Perhaps they didn't fit the target age or gender they were hoping to stockpile the jury with. It didn't matter.

....

The first candidate called into court was a man who appeared to be in his late 50s. He was asked whether he'd heard anything about the Candace Derksen case, including newspaper and television reports or even books written by family members.

"I certainly have, yes," he answered quickly.

The next question was whether he'd read or seen similar stories about the accused, Mark Grant.

"Yes I have," said the man.

Question three involved whether he recalled hearing any public statements by family members of the deceased teen.

"Not that I recall," he said after a brief pause.

The fourth, and final question, was the most important one. Did the man believe he had the ability to be impartial, or did his prior knowledge of the case compromise his judgment?

He took a few seconds before answering. "I believe it would be impacted, yes," he said.

Justice Joyal thanked him for his time and told him he was free to leave the courtroom.

Next up was exactly what justice officials were looking for. The elderly man was given the same set of questions and said he'd never heard of Candace Derksen or Mark Grant, therefore he'd have no difficulty keeping an open mind.

"This is what we want in a tryer. He'd be a perfect selection," said defence lawyer Saul Simmonds in approving the man to be the first of two "jury judges."

Next up was a middle-aged woman who admitted she knew quite a bit about the initial disappearance and discovery of Candace. However, she was in the dark about Mark Grant and hadn't followed any recent coverage of the case. Lawyers agreed she could become the second jury judge.

Now it was on to the main event.

....

The first potential candidate was a woman who appeared to be in her early forties. She admitted knowing a few details about Candace's killing but was unaware of any details about Mark Grant. She also couldn't recall hearing any statements from the Derksen family and declared no issues with being impartial.

The two jury judges consulted for a few seconds before declaring the woman was "unbiased." Crown attorney Brian Bell stood up and announced he had no objections. But defence lawyer Saul Simmonds had other ideas.

"Challenge," he announced. He didn't have to provide any further explanation for using his first of 20 challenges.

Justice Joyal explained to the woman that her services wouldn't be required. She appeared to be quite confused as she gathered her belongings and left the courtroom.

Up next was a young woman, perhaps in her late twenties. "I've seen some coverage about the case in the *Winnipeg Free Press*," she said. But the woman said the details were extremely limited and vague. She had no other knowledge of the case and told court she was ready to fulfill her public duty.

The two jury judges quickly declared her to be unbiased. Once again Bell stood up and announced he was satisfied with her ability to serve. This time, Simmonds followed suit. "Accepted," he said.

The Candace Derksen trial officially had its first juror seated.

....

The process would continue along the way for the next three hours and saw a total of 56 people screened in order to find a panel of 12 jurors and two alternates. Nearly half of the 42 who were rejected had actually disqualified themselves by presenting a litany of excuses as to why they couldn't participate. Some of them tested the patience of Justice Joyal.

"You're basically sabotaging your participation for reasons that aren't entirely sympathetic. That's not acceptable. Frankly, I feel that's a bit of an affront," Joyal told one young man who claimed he might have a tough time maintaining "emotional neutrality" based on the expected length of the trial.

"I feel a little freaked out," he said.

Many people expressed knowledge about the case, although that didn't result in an automatic rejection. The key issue was whether they could still hear the facts and render a verdict based solely on the evidence and not on pre-existing knowledge or beliefs.

Another man explained he couldn't afford to sit on a jury for more than 10 days because he was the only source of income in his family and time away from work would come out of his own pocket. Crown and defence lawyers agreed the man could be given a free pass. Joyal initially balked before agreeing. "Your reason is as predictable as night following day," he told the man before allowing him to leave.

Another older man made it clear he didn't want to be in court and claimed he once discussed particulars of

Candace's autopsy while on a hunting trip with another pathologist he knew. "You were prepared to say just about anything to get out of this, weren't you?" Joyal said before ordering him out of the courtroom.

Joyal ended up dismissing a total of 20 prospective jurors for a variety of reasons:

· Four expressed concerns about understanding English.

"My language not very good," one elderly Filipino man explained. When told he was being excused, he flashed a big grin at everyone in the courtroom. "Thank you everybody, good luck," he said.

"I'm almost sad to see him leave," Joyal said to laughter from the lawyers and public gallery.

· Four others raised the possibility they may have conflicts with potential witnesses who would be called to testify. In one case, a woman explained she had been at various social gatherings over the years with the former chief medical examiner who would provide key testimony about Candace's death.

· Four had major employment issues, which included not being compensated for their time on the jury.

· Four already upcoming holidays already purchased and paid for prior to receiving their jury notices.

· Four had medical issues such as high blood pressure and difficulty hearing.

"I really should avoid stress," said a middle-aged man, explaining he was on medication.

· Another eight potential jurors were deemed to be biased by the civilian jury judges and sent home.

In one case, a middle-aged woman said she had been following the case closely, including details about Mark Grant's 2007 arrest. "I hate to say this, but what I've read would make me think he's guilty based on the DNA," she admitted.

Another woman, appearing to be in her late 60s, began crying as she was asked whether she'd heard about Candace. "I would have real problems being impartial," she sobbed. The woman explained she had attended the same church as members of the Derksen family in the initial months following Candace's disappearance and slaying.

"You don't have to feel guilty about that," said Joyal. "I appreciate your honesty."

Later in the afternoon, another elderly woman admitted knowledge of the case and said she "possibly" could be unbiased. "Is that not the right answer?" she asked.

"There is no right or wrong answer," Joyal replied before dismissing her on the advice of the two civilian jury judges.

Another elderly man followed, saying he remembered the case "very, very well." When asked whether he could be impartial, he wasted no time in saying "I really don't think so."

By the end of the afternoon, defence lawyer Saul Simmonds had used 12 of his 20 challenges on jurors who had been deemed unbiased. Crown attorneys Brian Bell and Mike Himmelman had used just two.

With Simmonds, it appeared he was rejecting as many of the younger women who passed through the screening process as he could. Of his 12 challenges, nine were women who appeared to be in the 20-to-40-year-old age range. Perhaps he feared a jury stacked with that particular demographic would more easily relate to Candace's circumstances and be more likely to overlook the flaws in the Crown's case he was expecting to expose.

....

Every year, Manitoba Justice officials receive approximately 30,000 numbers from Manitoba Health Manitoba. The numbers correspond to residents of Winnipeg over the age of 18. All names are then placed in a private database. The extremely large pool will then be utilized for every jury trial to be held in the city over a 12-month period. Typically, only about 60 percent will even be contacted.

Jury selection is then held on a monthly basis, often with several panels being picked at a time. Justice officials match names to health care numbers and send out letters. The vast majority of people who respond are excused long before they even set foot into the courthouse. Normally, 1,600 summonses will be issued just to get a pool of 200 people to court. Jamie Krilyik, the provincial jury manager, says there are many reasons people will successfully apply for a statutory exemption.

Hardship cases may include people whose employers aren't obligated to pay them while they're on jury duty. Exemptions are also given to members of the justice system, elderly people who don't want to serve and members of religions that don't allow them to judge another person.

Other excuses don't carry as much weight. Krilyik has pretty much heard them all, including one man who said he couldn't carry out his civil duty because his home-made wine was going to be ready on a particular day and he had to stay home to bottle it. He was not granted an exemption.

Lindor Reynolds, a columnist with the *Winnipeg Free Press*, wrote an opinion piece critical of those who tried to shrug off serving on the Candace Derksen case.

> Very few people want to sit on a jury. It's inconvenient, pays poorly and takes up days or weeks of your life. You're not going to be featured in a Law and Order episode. But the only way an accused is guaranteed a fair jury trial is if the promised collection of his peers shows up," Reynolds wrote.
>
> The odds are against most of us serving on a jury. You might get a summons, but that's no guarantee you'll be listening to evidence and passing judgment. What is guaranteed is that our legal system cannot fairly do its work without average citizens stepping up and playing their part. This is your civic duty. It's something you should be prepared to do. If, God forbid, someone you know and love is on trial, you would want a jury of peers evaluating the evidence, weighing the facts and coming to an incontrovertible conclusion. You wouldn't want them to be judged by a handful of people who had plenty of spare time

and no job, family or obligations. Jury duty is inconvenient. The necessary parts of our lives often are.

The *Free Press* also ran an editorial, calling for a closer examination of the Canadian jury system based on the fact it appears to be growing increasingly difficult to get people motivated to serve. It read, in part:

The vast majority of people summoned for jury duty are usually excluded before they even get to court, resulting in the selection of juries from panels that fit a very narrow demographic—usually Caucasian, elderly, unemployed or retired. Aboriginals rarely serve.

Jury duty is a civic responsibility and at one time it was considered a privilege to sit on a panel that was called the "voice of the community." But the idea of jury duty as a privilege of citizenship has long since vanished.

The problem is not unique to Manitoba, but some jurisdictions have taken action to restore the sanctity of jury duty. New York state, for example, banned most exemptions in 1995, meaning lawyers, judges, doctors and politicians, who were previously excluded, had to serve.

As a result, heavyweights started showing up on juries, including then-mayor Rudolph Giuliani, actor Harvey Keitel and journalist Dan Rather. Lawyers usually don't like celebrities or intellectuals on juries, but the removal of most exemptions and excuses helped to restore the honour of serving on a jury.

Two of the biggest obstacles to jury duty are financial and time constraints. Jurors are paid $30 a day, starting on the 11th day. A judge can order special compensation in unusual circumstances, but for many people the cost of serving on a jury is too high.

Jury trials have also got longer in recent decades, often lasting several weeks and even months. The burden on workers and families is obvious.

The officials who manage Manitoba's jury system believe it is working, despite the widespread resistance by many of those who are asked to serve. The province should, however, conduct a study to determine how it can be improved and elevated, once again, to the voice of the community.

23

It was less than 48 hours before one of the most highly anticipated trials in Manitoba history was set to finally begin. Yet there remained a great amount of debate over what exactly the jury would be allowed to hear.

At issue was the bizarre story of Patricia Wilson. She was the young woman who claimed in 1985 that she was kidnapped by a stranger in eerily similar fashion to Candace Derksen. The investigation went cold and no arrests were ever made. But defence lawyer Saul Simmonds had come across the old file when preparing to defend Grant and immediately sought to have jurors hear about it.

He wanted to put Wilson on the stand on the grounds her story involved "similar fact evidence." He believed her story would prove Grant was innocent of killing Candace. That's because Grant was in custody on other charges at the time the woman, then just 12 years old, was allegedly attacked, meaning he couldn't possibly be responsible for either crime if there was indeed a proven link.

The Crown was vehemently opposed for one main reason—they believed Wilson was now claiming the abduction never actually happened.

Queen's Bench Justice Glenn Joyal was set to hear a full day of arguments on the issue, outside the presence of the jury in the form of a voir dire. He imposed a sweeping publication ban on the proceedings which extended through until the end of the trial.

Wilson, now 38, had been tracked down and re-interviewed by Winnipeg police only days earlier. They brought her to court on this day to testify in front of Joyal. It was clear this was pretty much the last place she wanted to be.

Wilson began crying within minutes of taking the witness stand. She answered a handful of basic questions, revealing she was now the mother of six children and had spent most of her life living in Winnipeg. Simmonds quickly switched the subject to her past.

Wilson was living with her parents in East Kildonan back in 1985, a student at Valley Gardens junior high. She recalled giving a statement to police some time that year. And that's where her memory apparently ended.

In a stunning development, Wilson was now claiming to have absolutely no idea what she spoke with police about. "I don't remember the details," she said through tears.

Simmonds began walking her through the original story presented to police. He reminded her about being discovered by a bystander in the fall of 1985 lying inside an empty railway car on Gateway Road in East Kildonan. She was screaming "Mommy, Mommy," her wrists and legs were bound and there was a plastic shopping bag put over her head.

Simmonds reminded Wilson how she told investigators that an unknown man had abducted her around 4 p.m. on a Friday as she left her school to walk home.

"I don't really recall the details," Wilson said repeatedly.

Simmonds wasn't giving up. He peppered her with a series of questions, asking for a description of the culprit, what type of vehicle he was driving, anything he said to her.

"I didn't know if my memories were dreams or real events," Wilson replied.

Simmonds asked Wilson if she wanted to read over her original police statement. She refused.

Simmonds continued. He asked Wilson about being brought by police to a memorial service held for Candace Derksen. He reminded her about investigators being on high alert, considering 13-year-old Candace had been snatched from her nearby East Kildonan school under similar circumstances. Police wanted her to scan the crowd for their potential attacker in case he was soaking in the public grief.

Still nothing.

"I don't have a lot of memories of my childhood," Wilson insisted.

Simmonds was growing increasingly impatient. He suggested Wilson was simply repeating what police officers had told her to say during their interview that had just occurred days earlier. He accused Wilson of recanting her story under instructions from police.

"On January 13, you told police that 'To the best of my knowledge it happened'," Simmonds said in reading from her statement.

Wilson said she now had more clarity, having spoken with family members, friends and even medical officials in the days that had passed. "I don't have any memories of that day," she said, crying.

Simmonds suggested she was actually "trying to forget that day." Wilson agreed. "I went through a lot of trauma as a child, had a lot of bad nightmares. I don't know whether some memories are nightmares or the truth," she explained. Simmonds seemed to accept this was as far as he was going to get with Wilson. He sat down.

Crown attorney Brian Bell began his cross-examination by getting straight to the heart of the issue. "I would suggest this never really happened," he said.

"I would agree, yes," Wilson replied.

Bell was done within two minutes.

Joyal had a few questions of his own. He asked Wilson when she first realized this incident never actually happened. Wilson said it was around the year 2000, shortly after her stepfather passed away. She didn't expand on her answer.

....

"This witness is obviously going through a serious trauma," Simmonds told Joyal during his argument on the issue. He said there were plenty of reasons her story should be put to the jury in the upcoming trial.

The distance between where Candace and Wilson were found was approximately five kilometres. There were Wrigley gum packages found at both scenes, a connection police were quick to make note of. Even the knot used to tie up Wilson's arms with plastic tubing was noted to be similar to the one found on the twine around Candace's arms.

"These are the kinds of similarities which should be called into court. Is (the gum wrapper) potentially a signature? The police certainly thought so," Simmonds argued. "We're talking about someone who would have to be a 12-year-old genius to create this kind of copycat situation."

He said there is no disputing Wilson was actually found in the rail car as described, because the independent witness who overheard her screams for help gave a statement in 1985. Unfortunately, that woman had since passed away. Simmonds said his client's "innocence was at stake" on this very important issue.

Bell told Joyal his decision was quite simple. With Wilson now under oath saying she wasn't abducted, there was no valid legal reason to put any of her previous story to the jury. "There was a very large investigation of this," said Bell. He said this issue would "derail" Grant's scheduled trial and had "no probative value."

Joyal took an adjournment to consider the issue. He returned to court on the morning of January 19—now less than 24 hours until the trial was set to begin—with his decision.

The jury would not hear about the "phantom kidnapper."

"I am not able to conclude ... the alleged offences even happened," he said.

....

There was another key piece of evidence that jurors weren't going to hear.

Crown attorney Brian Bell decided he was not going to call a woman who claimed Mark Grant confessed to the murder of Candace Derksen in 1988—only to retract his comments and threaten to harm a witness who overheard them. Bell was concerned about the reliability and credibility of Tania Lachance, especially since her story would appear to contradict that of another Crown witness who would be testifying.

Lachance had testified at Grant's preliminary hearing two years earlier, telling provincial court Judge Tim Preston about a conversation she had with Grant during a house party. Lachance, 38, was just 13 at the time Candace vanished in November 1984 and had previously gone to elementary school with her. She went by the last name of Walker at the time.

Years later, Lachance became friends with a girl in her Grade 10 class named Audrey Manulak. Grant was dating Manulak in 1988 when Lachance said she attended a house party on Talbot Avenue.

"We all started talking about the death of Candace," she said during the preliminary hearing. The conversation quickly turned serious when Grant allegedly interjected.

"Mark just came out and said 'I killed her,'" Lachance tes-tified. "And then, a couple minutes later he recanted it. He said 'I didn't do it, I'm just kidding, I'm just kidding.' We all just sat there. We didn't know what to say."

Lachance told court Grant and Manulak then began "fooling around in the living room … it was very sexual" while others looked on. That quickly cleared out the room.

Lachance said Grant and Manulak showed up at the door of her Moncton Avenue home the following night. "They threatened me, if I opened my mouth, that they would do to me what they did to Candace," Lachance testified. She said her father came to the door moments later, demanding the pair leave his property or he'd call the police. Lachance said she never saw Grant again, but Manulak became her next-door neighbour several years later.

"I was scared," she testified. "Never again was this talked about."

Lachance told court she stayed silent until police con-tacted her in 2008 after arresting Grant. She said Manulak provided information that led them to her. Manulak, for her part, was adamant that the conversations Lachance claimed happened were a figment of her imagination.

The issue of who was telling the truth was of no con-cern for the jury, however, since they weren't going to hear a peep about it until it hit the press following the trial.

24

It was a day they feared might never come. And one they couldn't wait to end. Such were the mixed emotions experienced by Cliff and Wilma Derksen as they settled into their front-row seats to watch the trial of their daughter's alleged killer finally begin.

Wilma had brought along a full supply of tissue, preparing for worst while hearing the Crown's opening statement. Cliff had brought along his sketchbook, as always, to put his emotions on paper.

They were surrounded by a large contingent of family members and friends who filled Winnipeg's largest courtroom to capacity, along with a throng of media and a handful of curious citizens who managed to find a seat.

Queen's Bench Justice Glenn Joyal gave nearly an hour's worth of instructions to the jury, explaining what was about to happen over the next several weeks. He urged them to listen intently, to focus only on the evidence presented in court and to avoid any media coverage of the high-profile case.

Prosecutor Mike Himmelman stepped up to the podium to formally open the case. He was reading from a carefully planned out script. Opening statements are meant to provide a template for jurors about what they are expected to hear and how the Crown plans to prove its case.

However, lawyers must always be careful in what they say. Speculation or commenting on evidence that may not ultimately be presented can prove to be fatal. No prosecutor wants to sink their own case and cause a mistrial before even calling their first witness.

"The charge is serious. But the evidence is fairly straightforward," Himmelman began. "Candace Derksen was alive when Grant tied her up. Because she died in the course of being forcibly confined, the charge is first-degree murder."

Jurors were told Candace succumbed to exposure to the elements and were shown several graphic photos of her body as it was found. They could see she was wearing a blue winter jacket, hooded sweatshirt, blouse and jeans. She was missing her right running shoe and her sock appeared to have been torn. A bag containing makeup, a clarinet and several school textbooks was also found in the shed.

The Crown planned to call more than 30 witnesses during the trial in what would prove to be an unpleasant trip down memory lane. They included former provincial medical examiner Dr. Peter Markesteyn, several scientists and forensic experts in the field of DNA evidence, the owner of the storage shed and the employee who found Candace's body, two of Candace's childhood friends, a convenience store clerk who was likely the last person to see Candace alive, Grant's six maternal siblings, police officers who originally interviewed Grant in December 1984, and the officer who arrested Grant in May 2007.

Retired Winnipeg police officer Ronald Allan was the first witness. He told jurors how investigators re-created the circumstances of Candace's death by tying up one officer in a similar fashion. "He could roll around on his back, front, side … but he was unable to stand up," said Allan.

It didn't take long for Grant's defence to become readily apparent. His lawyer, Saul Simmonds, was quick to pounce on Allan during cross-examination. Allan admitted nobody at the scene of the tragic discovery could have predicted the problem that lay ahead. After all, how do you preserve evidence you don't even know you've collected?

"You weren't in a position at that stage that the preservation of DNA was even a consideration, were you?" Simmonds asked.

Allan admitted the crime scene could have been "contaminated" after police found Candace's frozen body, her hands and legs bound with twine. He said investigators had no way of knowing at the time of scientific advances that were to come, allowing for forensic testing that would lead them to Grant more than two decades later.

"She was frozen stiff," Allan said.

Several officers walked through the shed and surrounding area, not wearing any protective clothing, masks or hairnets, as they collected about 40 exhibits, Allan told jurors. Those included seven strands of hair that had now been linked to Grant, found on a wooden stump.

"While you realize today you may have been contaminating things, you wouldn't have realized that back in 1985?" Simmonds asked.

"As far as things like hair and skin, no, we wouldn't," Allan replied. Allan couldn't say how many different sets of hands touched the twine from which Grant's DNA was ultimately extracted using advanced scientific techniques.

Simmonds suggested there was no way of knowing who the many officers at the scene previously had contact with, implying the possibility material was transferred to the scene. He asked Allan whether officers at the scene that day could have "coughed, sneezed ... scratched themselves" while searching for evidence.

Allan said it was possible, but the passage of time meant that there was no way to specifically remember.

. . . .

Darkness had fallen as the young woman walked out of the courthouse and headed to her car parked nearby. When she reached her vehicle, she was suddenly overcome with emotion. Tears began flowing from her eyes. The enormity of the task at hand washed over her. It had been a difficult few hours in the courtroom. There was still much work to be done.

She quickly managed to calm herself by focusing on what the Derksens had gone through. She had watched them closely during the day, drawing strength from the poise they showed while sitting through very difficult evidence.

"If they can get through more than 26 years of this, surely I can last six weeks," the juror thought to herself.

The woman drove off, knowing a difficult personal journey was only just beginning.

....

FRIDAY JANUARY 21, 2011

A playful schoolyard snowball fight. A giggling call home to her mother. And a short walk to her nearby residence with plans for a fun-filled weekend. Cliff and Wilma Derksen had spent years reliving every detail of their daughter's final day alive. Now a jury—and the public—was hearing about it for the first time.

"I remember sinking to my knees on the carpet at school, bawling my eyes out," David Wiebe testified about the exact moment he found out Candace was dead. He had been in class at Mennonite Brethren Collegiate Institute when the principal walked into their music room to inform students of the tragic discovery.

Under questioning from Crown and defence lawyers, Wiebe admitted to having a "crush" on Candace and was one of the last to see her alive. He recalled details of how the two engaged in a snowball fight just after 3 p.m. on the afternoon of November 30, 1984, which ended with Wiebe giving Candace a "face wash."

"She was just a fun, vibrant kid," said Wiebe. He then described how he watched Candace go to a phone and call her mother asking for a ride home.

Wilma cringed at this point of the testimony. Her biggest regret in life was now playing out in a public forum.

Jurors heard how Wilma had been home alone with her two younger children, getting the house ready for Candace's friend, Heidi, who was coming for a weekend sleepover.

Wilma had asked her daughter to make the short walk home, instead.

Wiebe said he watched as Candace headed east on Talbot Avenue, toward her residence on Herbert Avenue.

He never saw her again.

Wiebe testified he was shocked when a frantic Wilma Derksen showed up hours later at the school, asking Wiebe if he knew where Candace was. Wiebe was instantly concerned. "I told her I'm sure she'll show up. She had a worried look on her face," said Wiebe.

Winnipeg police were the next to show up, coming to Wiebe's residence that night and insisting he knew something about Derksen's whereabouts.

"This one officer kept saying how Candace was going to be home by midnight. He said, 'You know why? You're going to get in my car right now and take me to where she is'," Wiebe told jurors. "I just remember he was a really big cop. He kept saying that over and over again. And I just broke down, I kept saying I didn't know where she was."

Despite the accusatory tone, Wiebe said police never formally called him a suspect. He said the officer even issued an apology at the end of the questioning. "He said 'You know what David, I'm sorry I put you through this. I have to go question a couple more of Candace's friends like this'," Wiebe said.

He took jurors through details of his several statements to police, blood sample and his agreement to take a
polygraph in 2007 just before Grant was arrested. Wiebe
said he never hesitated to help.

"If I was the Derksens, I'd want people to be as coop-
erative as possible," he said. "The police told me they
wanted to eliminate anyone they'd interviewed before
they made an arrest."

Adis Avdi was the next to take the stand. He recalled
coming under similar suspicion. Avdi told jurors how
police suggested he might be responsible for graffiti in
the Elmwood neighbourhood near where Candace's body
was found, which included someone writing "Adis, if you
want Candace D you'll have to get through me first." The
message was near the Nairn overpass, a popular hangout
for kids in the area.

"As young kids, we spent a lot of time around that
area," said Avdi, who was just 12 at the time. He knew
Candace from elementary school. His family home
on Talbot Avenue was almost directly across from the
Derksen residence on Herbert Avenue.

"We used to all play tag, hide-and-seek, if it was winter we'd have snowball fights. You know, just a lot of
horsing around, horseplay," he said. "We'd spend a lot
of time by the train tracks, which we shouldn't have, but
we were, you know, just being kids."

Avdi said he wasn't the source of the message.

"I figured it was somebody just maybe pulling a prank,
because they knew me and Candace were good friends.

You know, maybe they were doing it to be mean. I don't know why that was written," he told jurors.

But police believed he might know more than he was admitting because he had seen Candace walking down Talbot that day as he drove by in a vehicle with his mother.

"We were going to visit my aunt. As we were driving down Talbot, I just happened to see her out of the corner of my eye. My mom knew her as well, so she honked. She waved at us and we waved back. That was pretty much it," said Avdi. He described Candace as a fun "tomboy" who seemingly got along well with everyone.

Avdi said his mother had initially contacted police to tell them about seeing Candace on her walk home, once word of her disappearance spread through the community like wildfire. He said police deemed him a "person of interest" at the time.

Blaine Webster also saw Candace on the day she disappeared when she came into the Redi Mart convenience store on Talbot. She asked to use the phone, and then left after about three minutes. Webster said he never heard the conversation but was surprised when police came the next day to search his property, which included a basement storage room and crawl space. They also asked him to take a polygraph but never followed through when he agreed.

Webster was asked if he'd ever seen Candace before.

"Yes. A lot of the kids come in for lunch and after-school snacks or treats, things like that. So, once this all occurred, and I pictured her, knew her face, I could recollect she had been in previously," he said.

Jurors also heard a statement from Victor Frankowski, the employee who found Candace's body while searching for a saw on the property. Frankowski had recently suffered a stroke and was unable to testify, but previously told officers he thought Candace "was a doll" when he found her lying face down in the shed. He immediately notified his boss, Frank Alsip.

"He was looking for some tools and upon entering the shed discovered the body," said former police officer Gilbert Clarke, who had taken the statement from Frankowski upon responding to the call.

Clarke said he immediately retreated from the scene and called for additional resources, never once entering the scene or touching anything inside.

"I saw a body lying on the floor. I wanted to preserve the scene for the identification unit," Clarke testified.

Former chief medical examiner Dr. Peter Markesteyn also took the stand, telling jurors how a hog-tied Candace may have been alive for up to 24 hours after being abandoned in -25 C weather. He said Candace likely didn't suffer any pain because she would have quickly gone unconscious. Her cause of death was hypothermia. There were no signs of sexual assault.

"The brain and organs can't function at such a low temperature. The brain doesn't send any messages to the heart and the heart stops," Markesteyn told jurors. "She lost consciousness pretty fast but it may have been hours before she died. There is no pain because the pain receptors no longer function. That is a sign things are getting worse, not better."

....

The day ended with Crown attorney Brian Bell reading a statement given by Wilma Derksen to police on January 23, 1985. Investigators who had just located Candace's body days earlier had asked Wilma to recall the details of the day her daughter disappeared.

Wilma bristled as Bell recited the words which were so familiar.

> *November 30 was pretty much a normal day for me. In the morning, I drove my husband to work at the Camp Arnes office and on the way we dropped Candace off at school. I went about my daily business. My nine-year-old was at school and the three-year-old was with the babysitter. I was home by 3:30 in the afternoon and just before 4 o'clock I received the phone call from Candace.*
>
> *Her phone call was a little late because she was normally home before the time she called. Candace would often call on Fridays if she knew I had the car because we would go shopping before we picked up her father. When we spoke on the phone, Candace first said "Hi, Mom" and then she giggled. She told me that Dave had just given her a face wash in the snow and she seemed happy. She asked me to pick her up at school and reminded me it was Friday.*
>
> *I told Candace that I couldn't pick her up because I was having problems with the two younger children. She said she wanted to come shopping that particular day because she was expecting a friend to visit for the weekend and she wanted to buy all the*

party foods like potato chips and pop. I told her that I would call her father and if he was getting off early I would drop by and get her. I called my husband but he had to stay at work until 5 o'clock.

Shortly after that, Candace phoned back and I asked her to walk home and said that way we could go out alone shopping during the evening. She said "Sure, Mom" and seemed to like the idea. She definitely wasn't upset about not getting a ride.

After the phone calls, I started cleaning up and didn't realize the time until about 4:40. I became concerned when Candace hadn't shown up yet and I bundled up the two younger children and drove over to the Camp Arnes office. We drove the route Candace takes home and were watching for Candace but didn't see her.

We stopped at the school and I checked the doors to find they were locked. I quickly picked up Cliff and we backtracked Candace's normal route home again. Again we didn't see her.

I was already getting worried and when we got home I phoned some of Candace's friends. I really can't remember exactly who I phoned or how many friends. While I was phoning, I think my husband went for a walk. When he got home again I think I told him I was real worried and I got in the car and drove back to the school. I was looking for David Wiebe, the boy who washed Candace's face. When I got to the school, I spoke to the principal and he pointed David out to me. David was in the hallway by his locker and I introduced myself and asked if he knew where Candace was. He said he didn't know and that he thought she went home. He appeared real shocked when I first met him and he must have thought I was there because of the face washing. I told him Candace wasn't home yet and he said that was terrible and he tried to comfort me because I was already starting to show emotion.

I went back home again and I think Cliff might have gone out for a walk to look around after that. I think it was shortly before 7 o'clock after all of my leads were exhausted that we phoned the police. Cliff was the one that actually called the police. After that, I stayed at home and prayed mostly. Somehow the younger children got to bed and sometime between 10 and 11 Cliff went out for a walk. It was sort of a frantic search on his part by then.

. . . .

They had survived the first two days of the trial, thanks to their family, their friends—and their faith. The same things that had got them through the past 26 years would no doubt carry them over these next few weeks.

Cliff and Wilma Derksen spoke openly outside court with media, describing the "surreal" atmosphere of a trial. *Free Press* columnist Lindor Reynolds wrote about their strength and courage they were displaying.

It would have been easy for Wilma and Cliff Derksen to hate, to let their grief fester and pock their remaining bitter days. Their lovely 13-year-old daughter was stolen, plain and simple. Instead, they did something unbelievable in the face of something unimaginable. They forgave, Reynolds wrote in her column.

The Derksens spoke openly about how prayer sustained them through the early days, when the search for Candace was ongoing and hope for a happy ending was quickly fading.

Wilma Derksen has to live with the guilt of refusing to pick up Candace from school that day. Forever, she will wish she'd jumped in the car and fetched the child. She and Cliff stayed strong, stayed dedicated to their marriage and remaining children. Many families don't, so buried in anger and sorrow, resigned to a life of prescription drugs or alcohol. Sometimes the sight of the other parent is a fresh, raw reminder of what was lost. Marriages end. Sorrow moves in, wrote Reynolds.

Cliff and Wilma knew there were still many challenges ahead. Much of the evidence would be painful to hear. The fate of Mark Grant was very much up in the air. Their odyssey through the justice system might only just be starting.

Over the next weeks, the Derksens will be forced to relive every moment of their daughter's abduction and death. Clinical and precise words will not erase the pain. They believe in heaven and in forgiveness, too. Their daughter was placed, however temporarily, in hell. They have reconciled that, too. As the roll call of experts testifies, as the terrible details are brought to light, as facts as small as Candace being found with her clarinet emerge, their pain will be renewed, wrote Reynolds.

But they will endure. As Mark Edward Grant's first-degree murder trial continues, as more evidence is placed on the record, they will stay strong. After losing their eldest child, nothing can hurt as much. They're tough, these parents, because they've had to be. They're tough because their faith allows them to share the burden.

25

His DNA may have been linked to the Candace Derksen killing, giving prosecutors what they believed was a scientific "smoking gun," but it was becoming increasingly clear the first-degree murder case against Mark Grant was going to be anything but routine.

Defence lawyer Saul Simmonds was making a clear effort to raise a doubt about the validity of the forensic evidence in the first few days of the trial. A spoiled crime scene, sloppy police work and the erosion of memories through the passage of time were all becoming recurring themes. Whether it was having an impact on the 12-person jury remained to be seen.

On this day, Simmonds asked a flurry of questions of several witnesses who took the stand while raising a number of possible theories—including that Grant may have once worked at the business where Candace's body was found.

Property owner Frank Alsip said the shed where Candace's body was found had come from Beausejour, a small town just east of Winnipeg. He had also taken a look at the body prior to police arriving but stayed outside the shed the entire time. Under cross examination,

Simmonds questioned whether Grant may have ever worked for him. Alsip, who employed about 15 workers at the time, said the name or face wasn't familiar. But he admitted all employment records from that era had been destroyed years ago.

"So you couldn't say if Mark Grant worked for you, even if for just a short time?" asked Simmonds. Alsip agreed he could not.

"Realistically, you're relying on your memory. Is that correct, sir?" said Simmonds.

"Correct," Alsip replied.

"And whether or not he was so employed you couldn't tell me that today. It would be impossible. Is that fair?" Simmonds continued.

"That's fair," Alsip answered.

Alsip admitted he had no video surveillance of the property, which was a popular destination for trespassers and transients.

"Unfortunately people were free to come and go as they chose, weren't they?" he asked. Alsip said that was true.

"The odd time, you know, kids would fool around on weekends and whatnot, no question. We eventually did put up a fence to stop the damage that started to happen from the neighbourhood kids," he said.

Alsip told jurors he seemed to recall an old jacket covering Candace's body when she was found. Yet none of the police officers who attended the scene recalled such an item, and no jacket was ever seized. "I could see the body with the head away from me, and an old parka that had been in the building left from an employee that worked in Beausejour had been put on top of the body," he said.

Alsip said police had briefly searched the area surrounding his property on December 30th, 1984. He also recalled the City of Winnipeg was storing thousands of sandbags on his property at the time. They were all secured with twine, similar to what was used to bind Candace inside the shed.

"You have no idea how many people may have come in contact with that twine, do you?" asked Simmonds.

"No, I don't," said Alsip.

....

A similar line of questioning was put to several police officers who attended the scene. Of course, every Crown witness to date had no memory of a previous meeting with Grant, which would seem to rule out the possibility of an inadvertent transfer of DNA evidence. But Simmonds appeared to be leaving that door open by asking specific questions to officers about whether they could recall every person they encountered, meal they ate, grocery store they shopped at or movie they watched in the weeks preceding the investigation.

None could, of course. But that was not the point of this exercise. Simmonds only had to raise a "reasonable doubt" in the minds of jurors. And since all 12 had to be unanimous in their verdict, it would only take one reluctant juror to sink the Crown's case.

Robert Parker was a long-time member of the police identification who retired in 2009 as an inspector. He attended the crime scene on January 17th, 1985 and took a number of photographs now entered as exhibits. He worked on the case under the supervision of Sgt. Wayne Bellingham, who died of cancer a few years earlier and was unable to testify. Parker's grim assignment had included following Candace's body to Seven Oaks Hospital and documenting the process with his camera.

"The victim was placed on a gurney, and the photographs were taken at that time. She was in a shroud, and the hands and the head had been covered with paper bags," Parker testified. He explained that the bags were placed on Candace by another identification officer to assist with preservation of any potential evidence.

Parker described the various items of clothing Candace was found in and how they were removed, bagged, photographed and marked. He returned to Seven Oaks three days later to photograph the autopsy that was done on Candace. The process was initially delayed to allow for her body to thaw. He led jurors through a series of pictures which documented the process. It was a difficult experience for everyone in the courtroom.

....

As the first full week of the trial continued, testimony became increasingly scientific. Donald Olgivie took the witness stand, telling jurors how he analyzed five exhibits that were given to him by police in 1988. Ogilvie was working at the time as the hair and fibre analyst with the RCMP. His career would take him across much of the country, including more than 150 courtrooms to testify as an expert witness. He eventually moved to Australia to head up a crime lab before retiring in 2008.

Ogilvie said a total of 52 hairs were collected—24 from a jacket Candace was found wearing, 22 from her blue jeans, four from the twine, one from her sock and one from a log found near her body. Of those, seven were set aside because of similarities between them.

"Back in those days, you weren't even aware of the possibility of DNA contamination, were you?" Simmonds asked. Ogilvie couldn't be sure if he wore gloves to handle the samples and said it was theoretically possible that there was a transfer of secondary DNA to the test sample. "It's not like the TV show CSI at all," said Ogilvie. He said police gave him two samples of twine, each secured in a plastic evidence bag.

Another witness, Robert Chisnall, made similar admissions. He was an expert in ligatures and knots and was asked to analyze the twine used to bind Candace. Chisnall said police gave him a total of 14-feet worth of twine in September 1988. He kept the exhibit for about a month before returning it to investigators. Chisnall said he handled the twine multiple times without gloves and would have laid it on a table that hadn't been bleached.

"Back in the day, you weren't even aware of the possibility of DNA contamination?" asked Simmonds.

"It's a much different practice now," Chisnall admitted under cross examination.

Simmonds asked whether Chisnall may have inadvertently transferred DNA on the twine during examination.

"It's theoretically possible," he replied.

Simmonds began to speak about various wrongful conviction cases in Canada where forensic testing had been a central issue. Crown attorney Brian Bell jumped up to object, forcing Justice Glenn Joyal to send jurors out of the room. "It's highly prejudicial if my friend is able to make such reference," Bell pleaded.

Joyal agreed. "Keep the jury focused on the issues they can consider," he told Simmonds.

....

Pamela Dixon, who worked at the RCMP forensic lab in Ottawa, admitted stringent procedures now in place to deal with forensic evidence were not followed in the Candace Derksen investigation. In fact, Dixon had authored a national report years earlier which called on all crime scene investigators to wear masks, gloves, protective suits—even two pairs of rubber gloves.

Simmonds asked if "a whole bunch of people, over the years, touching things without gloves, possibly coughing, sneezing on it" could have impacted the integrity of the evidence linked to his client.

"There is a possibility, yes," Dixon told jurors. However, she said if foreign DNA was introduced to the exhibit, there would be been multiple profiles gathered by investigators.

Dixon was assigned in 2001 to deal with the case, which involved extracting DNA from seven pieces of the twine used to bind the teen's body. She described the intricate process to jurors, which includes several chemical treatments used to separate biological material from the exhibit. Just over 10 nanograms of DNA were collected in total, court was told. A nanogram is defined as one-billionth of a gram. "It's such an infinitesimal amount that most of us can't even comprehend it,' said Simmonds. Dixon agreed, but said she amplified the DNA in order to create a profile that was eventually forwarded to police.

....

Winnipeg Police Service Sgt. John Burchill testified how he became involved in the case in early 2001. That's when he sent a small cardboard box containing the twine to RCMP for forensic testing. Under cross-examination by Simmonds, Burchill said he did not know how many people had handled the twine before going to the RCMP lab. "It certainly wasn't packaged as I expected," he said.

Court also heard that RCMP tested gum and other items connected to the scene, like a chip bag. Police also kept the shed in which Candace's body was found, he said. With much of the forensic evidence out of the way, the Crown was now preparing to move into a new phase of their case. Jurors were about to get inside the head of Mark Grant around the time he allegedly killed Candace.

....

She was a 14-year-old runaway full of rebellion and looking for adventure. Now, 27 years later, she was a middle-aged woman, filled with regret about her time spent with Mark Grant. Audrey Fontaine (formerly Audrey

Manulak) took the witness stand, called by the Crown to share details about her time spent with Grant beginning with their first meeting in the summer of 1984.

Fontaine told jurors she met Grant on the streets after taking off from her parents. She said they started out hanging out together, drinking beer and smoking marijuana. The first two nights they spent together was "in a hole in the ground," a cement underground chamber near the Higgins Avenue railway yards off Main Street. "It was like a large room with pipes in it," Fontaine said. "He had a hot plate and a ghetto blaster." They next stayed with his father at a downtown apartment.

"We had a relationship," she told defence lawyer Saul Simmonds during cross-examination. "He didn't hold me captive."

Fontaine said their relationship ended once Grant was arrested on unrelated charges just a few days after Candace disappeared. "We were close," she told Simmonds, "but he wasn't with me when he was arrested."

Fontaine testified she remembered seeing Candace once in a corner store on Talbot Avenue. Both went to different schools but it was that link that initially led police to question Grant in late 1984.

Another former friend of Grant told court how he would often come over to his Talbot Avenue residence to "drink and party" around the time of Candace's killing. "We would go to the bar and invite the bar over," said William Crockford. "The parties would last for one or two days."

Menno Zacharias, then with the youth division, told jurors that he and another officer only spoke to Grant to check out the veracity of a tip from Fontaine about Candace's disappearance. "He wasn't a suspect in the case," Zacharias testified. He said Grant told officers he didn't know the 13-year-old missing girl.

Zacharias said Fontaine had told police she saw Candace after her disappearance. Zacharias said police weren't convinced she was being truthful and spoke to Grant about it. Fontaine also voluntarily submitted to a polygraph test. "It was very straightforward," Zacharias, a former deputy police chief who is now retired, said of the 23-minute interview. "There was no animosity on his part."

Zacharias said police interviewed Grant when he was an inmate at the Winnipeg Remand Centre. Grant was being held for being unlawfully at large on an unrelated charge. Grant told the officers he had recently dyed his hair before his arrest. He also admitted to spending a few nights with Fontaine in the underground inspection pit in the CPR Weston rail yards, about six kilometres from where Candace was found. The interview ended. It would be more than two decades before police would talk to Grant again.

26

It's often called the CSI effect. And it has become a major concern to police and prosecutors across North America. Popular prime time TV shows have tricked much of the general public into believing that forensic science is as glitzy and fast-paced as it's often portrayed in a one-hour drama.

Of course, DNA analysis is a much more complex and painstakingly slow process. Forget about getting the results by the next commercial break. It can often take months to get evidence examined and processed. Judges now routinely speak to jurors about lowering their expectations when it comes to this type of evidence. And now the parade of expert witnesses at the Candace Derksen trial offered a similar caveat as they took the stand.

Sgt. Jon Lutz was the next in line, explaining to jurors how the seven tiny hairs found at the initial crime scene proved to be a major break in the case. Lutz, a former member of the Winnipeg police cold case unit, had started reviewing the cold case in early 2006 and saw Mark Grant's name on the list of people who'd been interviewed by police. "There were no standout suspects on the initial read of the file," he testified.

But all that changed in November 2006 when officers re-interviewed Audrey Fontaine about her involvement with Grant around the time of the murder. "Based on that conversation, we decided that we wanted to talk again to Mark Grant," said Lutz.

To obtain a warrant, build a case against Grant, they'd need to determine if his DNA was a match to the hair/fibre samples from the original crime scene, which could now be subjected to much more sophisticated testing. On November 23, 2006—almost 22 years to the day after Candace vanished—Lutz sent the hair samples which had been in storage to Molecular World in Thunder Bay.

Lutz explained how the hairs were recovered from Candace's jacket, kangaroo sweater, right sock and on a stump that was inside the wooden shed. "I thought it was kind of strange that they were all over the place," Lutz told jurors.

He said results of that analysis narrowed the police service's reopened investigation of case. Lutz explained how officers had previously looked at convicted killer Stanley Pomfret as a possible suspect. Jurors were told how Pomfret killed Tena Franks and raped two other girls in the early 1990s, but he was ultimately ruled out as a suspect in the Candace Derksen case.

After they obtained a sample of Grant's DNA police sent it to the Thunder Bay lab for testing in early January 2007. They got their results about two weeks later. "We decided we needed to start a short-term task force," Lutz said. They assigned the name of "Project Angel" to the case, with Grant now their primary target.

One of the first objectives was to set up a special surveillance unit in order to obtain a "discarded DNA sample," Lutz said. He also described how police had to begin
connecting Grant's family tree, a painstaking process that
lasted several months.

....

It was a bizarre place to have a family reunion. Then
again, there was nothing typical about the situation Mark
Grant's maternal siblings now found themselves facing.

The Crown had arranged for five family members
to fly to Winnipeg and testify at Grant's trial, each one
taking just a few minutes on the stand. The Crown simply wanted to cover their bases by showing jurors the
DNA evidence couldn't have come from anyone but
Grant himself.

The move was also necessary because defence lawyer
Saul Simmonds didn't want to simply concede the fact
that all of these witnesses were born to the same mother.
"A whole bunch of these people didn't even know about
each other. They're all relying on hearsay as to where they
came from," said Simmonds.

The unusual comment drew a chuckle from Crown
attorney Mike Himmelman. "Isn't it hearsay, to some
extent, for all of us in terms of how we find out where
we come from?"

Complicating matters was the fact that the head of
the family, Gloria Caverley, could not testify because she
had died in 2009. Jurors heard how Caverley had seven
children by five different men, with many of them not

even knowing each other until the criminal investigation surfaced. For most, the first time they'd ever been in the same room as their stepbrother was when they entered court. "Welcome to Winnipeg," Joyal said in an attempt to lighten the mood.

First up was Katherine Cole, who had spent all of her life living in British Columbia. This was her first time ever visiting Winnipeg, hardly under ideal circumstances. "I've been told we are related, but before this I didn't know that. It was completely unknown to me," she told jurors.

Frank Cole was next, telling a similar story of growing up on the West Coast and not learning his mother had other children until 2007. "It was when the police showed up at my door," he said. "Now I know of (Grant), but I don't know him."

All the family members tracked down by police had provided DNA samples and were co-operative with the investigation. All but one had been living out of province at the time of Candace's slaying and had alibis which checked out with police.

"I've never met him but I've heard of him now," Grant's stepsister, Rhonda Wiens, told jurors.

Deborah Barker, who was the only sibling that also shared the same father as Grant, explained how they were abandoned by their mother as children. "I never knew my mother," she said, sadly. She had also lost contact with Grant years earlier, believing he was still going by the name of Mark Barker. She, too, had no idea that her mother went on to have several other children until police notified her. "I heard throughout time of other possibilities but never knew," she said.

John Barker was the final sibling to take the stand. He shared at least one thing in common with Grant—a criminal past. Barker was escorted to court by police because he was still a sentenced prisoner. Jurors weren't told any specifics about his past. Like everyone else but Deborah Barker, he had never met Grant. "I believe he's my stepbrother. Same mother, different father," he said.

Simmonds wanted to make a deliberate point with all of the witnesses, suggesting to them that Caverley may have even had other children she never told them about prior to her death. "How many other secrets were kept from you, you wouldn't know," he said.

....

With the family tree now planted for jurors, the trial shifted back to the lab. Curtis Hildebrandt, a senior scientist with Molecular World in Thunder Bay, was next to testify. He explained how the hairs found in the shed had mitochondrial DNA common to Grant and seven of his siblings. "Essentially, they look the same," said Hildebrandt. He said specific DNA profiles were developed from each hair sample. Mitochondrial DNA is passed to children exclusively from the mother so that all children of the same mother have the same mitochondrial DNA.

Arlene Lahti, a former senior scientist with Molecular World, told jurors she processed DNA samples from 10 individuals, including seven of Grant's brothers and sisters, his ex-girlfriend Audrey Fontaine, convicted killer-rapist Stanley Promfet and Candace's school friend, David Wiebe. The lab found that Fontaine's, Pomfret's and Wiebe's DNA did not match the DNA of Grant, his siblings and the hair found in the shed.

Defence lawyer Saul Simmonds grilled Hildebrandt and Lahti on procedures used by the lab to test the hair samples, and on the process used to test the twine that bound Candace. Under cross-examination, Hildebrandt said in testing the twine—using material supplied by the RCMP from an earlier DNA test—the sample ended up being destroyed. He told jurors the test was a last-shot attempt at developing a DNA profile from the material and that he had permission from Winnipeg police.

"I do not believe we breached the guidelines," Hildebrandt told Simmonds. "This is the last chance we have for extracting that material. We thought it was appropriate to try to develop a profile."

Jurors had already heard DNA linked to Grant was found on the twine. But Simmonds argued that in destroying the evidence, it could no longer be tested by another lab for independent verification. He also suggested there was a financial motive for Hildebrant's company to see their work end in success. "How well the company does makes a difference to you ... not just financially, but personally," Simmonds said.

The Crown's next witness was Amarjit Chahal, the head of the Thunder Bay lab. He said only one person in 50 million would have the same DNA as that found on twine used to bind Candace before her death. Chahal spent nearly two days on the witness stand, trying to explain the complex process while defending the lab's practices and even his own credentials.

Crown attorney Brian Bell, Chief Justice Glenn Joyal and defence counsel Saul Simmonds had to ask Chahal the same question more than once. At least once, Bell corrected Chahal about a statistic and, at one point, the judge called a recess to allow Chahal time to examine his reports. Simmonds questioned the scientist about his resume and expertise. Chahal admitted that both his undergraduate and graduate degrees were in plant sciences.

He said that during his education, and at his previous employment, he didn't do DNA testing for forensic purposes. He also said that of the hundreds of forensic cases his DNA laboratory had examined, probably only about five to 10 involved degraded samples of DNA such as in the Grant case.

Simmonds repeatedly grilled Chahal about the reliability of his lab's findings. He also questioned Chahal about what the lawyer claimed were some lapses in recording information, unscientific methods for ignoring some of the findings, and a failure to ask police to forward more samples from other people. "You started manipulating the data until it gave you a basis for inclusion, didn't you?" said Simmonds.

Chahal agreed with Simmonds that the laboratory didn't request a sample from the body of Candace to test, and it also didn't test samples from 11 police and forensic personnel who touched the samples or were around them. Because of that, Chahal admitted he couldn't say whether the hair tested for DNA analysis was Candace's, and he also agreed the seven hairs—found in different places in the shed where Candace's body was discovered—could be from seven different people because of the limitations of the testing technology on DNA that comes from degraded samples. "This is not pristine DNA," he said. "This is degraded DNA … it is not normal DNA," he said.

It was difficult to gauge just how much of this scientific evidence was being digested by jurors. And, most importantly, whether it was casting doubt in their minds about whether the right man was even on trial. The trial was about to take a sharp 180 degree turn. Jurors would move from the science labs to the police interrogation room—and hear directly from the man on trial.

....

He appeared unemotional and repeatedly professed his innocence—even after being confronted with his DNA evidence being found at the crime scene.

"I've got nothing to say about that," a clearly unimpressed Mark Grant told Sgt. Al Bradbury and Sgt. Jon Lutz on a three-hour videotaped interview now being played for jurors. It was recorded on the day of his May 2007 arrest at the Public Safety Building in downtown Winnipeg. "I didn't know her. If you guys have a case, then prove it to me because I don't believe you do."

"Most people know something about her," Lutz shot back. "You may be the only person who doesn't."

Bradbury took the witness stand to help take jurors through Grant's statement. He was slated to be the final Crown witness. Jurors watched as the officers tried repeatedly to get Grant to confess without success.

"I'm not going to put any sort of pressure on you or anything like that," Bradbury told Grant on the tape. "But if you choose to explain what happened on that day—it's not my job to judge you or anything like that. I'll sit here. I'll listen. I don't know, maybe you have some overwhelming urges that you can't control that have led to this."

Lutz asked Grant if perhaps Candace's death was an accident or a prank gone wrong. "You can't really tell people what's causing a lot of that unrest in you," Lutz said. "I can't imagine really having to hold onto something like that for all those years and not being able to find an outlet for that."

Grant remained silent. "I have nothing more to say," he told the officers, his tattooed arms folded against his chest. Grant's demeanour changed when the officers, late in the interview, finally confronted him with the DNA evidence. Grant hung his head in silence, refusing to look at the officers.

"We built a case on the fact that we're saying you're the murderer in this situation," Bradbury said. "That forensically, scientifically we are going to prove our case. You say you don't know Candace, you've never been there, there's no reason for your DNA to be there. We say that's because you're the murderer."

The officers also told Grant that it took Candace about 30 hours to freeze to death, and that she would have likely gone in and out of consciousness. They were trying to provoke Grant. "Apparently, it's a very painful death," Lutz said.

"I don't know if somebody can get gratification by standing over that body, by looking at it tied up like that," Bradbury added. "Is that a possibility somebody can get gratification from that?"

Grant quickly rejected that theory. "I don't experience stuff like that 'cause I didn't do it, whether you want to believe it or not," he told the officers. He also claimed he didn't even know the location of Nairn Avenue—the well-known Winnipeg thoroughfare close to where Candace's body was found.

"Forty-three years old, you've been living in Winnipeg all your life and you don't know the (Nairn overpass)?" Lutz said.

Bradbury told jurors how they interviewed Grant off-and-on for about 16 hours. During cross-examination, he defended both the interrogation and police investigation. "My purpose in there is to try to the find the truth," he told jurors. He said the initial re-investigation included several possible theories, including one in which Candace died as a result of a prank gone horribly wrong. "We kept as wide as scope as we could at all times," Bradbury told defence lawyer Saul Simmonds. He said Grant became the only suspect once lab analysis showed forensic evidence found at the scene could only have come from Grant.

"It's time to find out the whys. We know who did what. We know where it was happening. The why. We say you left her there. She died as a result of that. That's first-degree murder. This is your chance to spin it, you want to tell me the truth, let me know, or let the science talk," Bradbury said to Grant during the interview.

"No comment," Grant shot back.

"No comment?" said Bradbury.

"No," Grant quickly replied.

"How can you not comment about a girl that died, left there?" asked Bradbury.

"I'm just going on my lawyer's advice," Grant explained.

"That's great. Your lawyer's advice, so you fully understand all that. You understand science too, right, Mark?" said Bradbury, his tone becoming more aggressive.

"Well, science has been known to be wrong," Grant replied.

"So it's got to be the science that's wrong 'cause that can't be your hair there? That can't be your biological substances there?" asked Bradbury.

"No," said Grant.

"No?" Bradbury repeated.

"No comment," Grant said angrily

The interview was over. And the Crown's case was now complete.

27

The Crown had rested. Now it was up to Mark Grant's defence to take their final shot at picking apart the case against their client. In the process, they had made an intriguing tactical decision. Grant would give up his right to have the final word to the jury in exchange for them calling their own expert witness to testify. Normally, the Crown is first to make a closing argument, followed by the defence. But the roles reverse if the defence chooses to call evidence.

Simmonds had weighed the pros and cons of such a decision, but ultimately figured he needed someone who could attempt to refute some of the Crown's scientific case against Grant. He found just the witness in Dr. John Waye, a genetics professor at McMaster University in Ontario. Under direct questioning, Waye was quick to condemn some of the science used to link Grant to Candace Derksen's killing.

In his most blunt assessment, Waye told jurors "bad science" was behind some of the DNA analysis done by the Thunder Bay lab that linked biological material found at the scene and on Candace's clothing to Grant. "You're looking at the profile of Mr. Grant being a contributor and you're covering up all the evidence that disagrees with that," Waye said in describing the lab's analysis of DNA samples provided by the Winnipeg Police Service. "You can't ignore data because it doesn't fit your expectations."

Jurors also heard how Waye had worked with the RCMP and testified in several high-profile criminal cases involving DNA, including that of B.C. serial killer Robert Pickton. He had spent considerable time reviewing the Crown's case against Grant. Waye said he wasn't critical of all the lab work the Thunder Bay lab did, just three specific elements. "Parts of the data fit. Parts of the data he doesn't fit," he said.

Crown attorney Brian Bell cross-examined Waye on many of his findings, which he admitted were based largely on opinion. Once Waye was off the stand, Simmonds announced he was calling no additional witnesses. The stage was set for closing arguments.

. . . .

WEDNESDAY FEBRUARY 16, 2011

"Bad science." Saul Simmonds began his final pitch to the jury with those two words. He paused for effect, allowing them to linger in the air. He followed with several others. "Ignored evidence … evidence that is tainted."

As many expected, the veteran defence lawyer repeatedly told jurors how police overlooked certain evidence that pointed away from Grant, contaminated the original crime scene and mishandled key exhibits such as the twine used to tie Candace Derksen up. "You must have been wondering for weeks where is the evidence, how did we get here?" he told jurors. "This is a case with overwhelming doubt. Einstein warned against what is bad science."

He suggested the real killer had never been caught and what really happened to Candace remained an unsolved mystery. "What happened in that shed? Was it a prank? Was it a game played by some that ended tragically? Was she taken by someone? Those answers we will never know," said Simmonds. He said the case reminded him of "Alice In Wonderland … where up is down and down is up. And off with their heads, says the Red Queen," said Simmonds.

Simmonds explained why he called an expert witness in an attempt to discredit some of the DNA findings used against his client. He made sure to point out to jurors the move meant he gave up his right to have the final word. "When in argument you always want to have last word. But I wanted you to hear from a real scientist," Simmonds said during his 75-minute final address. He argued that police "went down every rabbit hole they could" in trying to make the evidence fit against Grant, saying they wanted them to "ignore evidence of the innocence of a man and sweep it under the carpet."

"In 1985 there were no controls, no real efforts for the preservation of DNA," he said. Simmonds then tried an analogy that any good Canadian could relate to—hockey. He said you would never play an entire season, only to "change the rules" during overtime of Game 7 of the Stanley Cup. Simmonds suggested that's exactly what the Crown was now asking jurors to do in relation to this "tainted" investigation. "A man should look for what is, not what he thinks should be," he said.

Simmonds spoke of three pieces of chewing gum found inside the shed. Only one was linked to Candace. The other two didn't contain Grant's DNA. Same went for the empty bag of chips found discarded near her body. "Who was eating taco chips with Candace Derksen? Who was chewing gum with Candace Derksen? It wasn't Mark Grant," said Simmonds.

He said Grant was no "criminal mastermind," just a simple man who had been linked to a notorious case which turned the arresting police officers into "celebrities."

"This case is fraught with contamination. Your responsibility is to protect him from a possible wrongful conviction. He is not the person who did this. His future now rests in your hands."

....

Queen's Bench Justice Glenn Joyal ordered a 20-minute recess. Mark Grant was taken back into the lockup area while the majority of the spectators stayed behind in the courtroom, not wanting to risk losing their seat in the jam-packed gallery.

Simmonds's powerful final pitch had created a buzz. Even members of the Derksen family admitted to their legion of supporters they were impressed by his tone and delivery. Now the big question was how jurors would react.

Cliff and Wilma Derksen believed the case against Grant was strong. But they also believed Simmonds had made a very convincing attempt to raise some doubts.

Would it be enough? There was some comfort in know-
ing Crown attorney Brian Bell had yet to take the floor.
They had confidence in his ability to rectify any damage
Simmonds had done.

....

Brian Bell was direct and to the point. He told jurors their
job was relatively simple if they ignored the "red herrings"
being thrown their way. He assured jurors there should be
no dispute about Grant's guilt. He said the DNA evidence
clearly connected Grant to the slaying; and reminded
them of the one-in-50-million chance the genetic profile
was from someone else. He said there was no reasonable
explanation for Grant's DNA at the crime scene if he didn't
commit the crime.

"Please don't speculate on things you don't know,
focus on what you do know," said Bell in a calm, mea-
sured tone. Yes, several police officers had admitted to
handling certain evidence, including the twine in question,
without wearing gloves or other protective equipment
because the concept of DNA testing didn't exist in 1985.
But Bell said that didn't change the fact Grant was found
to be a perfect match. He urged jurors to ignore claims
by Simmonds that it was possible Grant may have previously worked at the brickyard where her body was located. "There is no evidence he did work there," said Bell.

He said there was no question this was a first-degree
murder, given that Candace was killed during the course
of a confinement. "The only issue is who tied her up,"
he said.

Bell accused Grant of trying to confuse the evidence to distract them from the truth. One example was when Simmonds noted three pieces of chewing gum and a bag of chips were found in the shed near her body, with no DNA connected to Grant. Bell said those items could have been inside the shed long before her body was and have nothing to do with the case. "He hog-tied Candace Derksen and left her to die. You'll come to one conclusion and one conclusion only," said Bell.

....

It was shortly after noon when both lawyers had completed their final arguments. Justice Glenn Joyal dismissed jurors for lunch but asked them to return to court by 2 p.m. He had warned them it was going to be a long day. He then spent the remainder of the afternoon going through a detailed reading of the law, explaining to jurors the importance of carefully considering all the evidence. "Keep an open mind but not an open head" when deliberating, Joyal said.

Joyal also outlined four possible verdicts—first-degree murder, second-degree murder, manslaughter, or not guilty. He spent considerable time explaining the definition of each offence and how the evidence would have to apply to reach a verdict on each.

It was about 5 p.m. when Joyal concluded his charge to the jury. He urged them not to jump to any quick conclusions, to spend as much time as necessary going through the weeks of evidence and carefully considering their very important task. The jurors had brought overnight bags with them to court, as they would not be allowed to return home until their deliberations were over.

The case was in their hands. Now the waiting game began.

....

The Derksen family had set up inside the Law Courts, preparing for what could be a lengthy process. They were gathered inside a newly-renovated room meant for victim of crime and their families. This would be their home away from home until a verdict was reached. As long as the jury was deliberating, they didn't plan to stray very far.

Wilma Derksen had plenty of thoughts bottled up inside, a myriad of emotions pouring through her. As always, she found solace in writing out what was on her mind. She posted the following on her blog.

How am I doing?

I don't know.

"Convince me." That's what I wanted. The last day of the trial, I wanted to be convinced one way or the other without any reasonable doubt. I think that's what we all wanted as we listened to the closing arguments by both defence and Crown Wednesday.

"Bad science," were the defence's words as he summed up his argument.

"DNA says he was present," was the Crown's summation.

And the judge talked forever about how the jurors were to arrive at their decision. "Use your common sense," he said in the end.

I don't envy them.

It was all brilliant. We've definitely had three of the best minds deliberating over it all.

For me it was worth it all as again another piece of the puzzle slipped into place. That one little piece of new insight was worth it all, as we have sat there endlessly for almost five weeks now.

Candace was worth it. My children need to hear it. I am grateful for every word spoken.

But these keepers of the truth are all lawyers with lawyer ways. I wanted story—not facts.

I wanted all the pieces of the puzzle to be laid out and then pulled together into a beautiful story with character development, main plot, subplots, climax, descriptions, and a grand finale with good winning in the battle of good and evil, the truth in drama not more legalese.

As someone left, I heard him mutter, "I'll wait for the movie."

Actually, now that it is done, I think I want to wait for the movie, too. I want it not only all figured out but also done in a style that is easily accessible. I want story. I want to know the answer to the elusive "why?"

And I want someone to write it out for me in a way I understand. It could begin, "As Candace was walking home that fateful day, an unknown man came up behind her. It was snowing, the visibility was poor. She didn't know him and was surprised at his forwardness as he started to engage her in a conversation ... Before she knew it ... His name was..."

Then I want the story to continue for the next 26 years ending with the conclusion, "And the jury's decision was..."

The reality is I don't know if we will ever know the details I am looking for. This isn't the forum to provide that for me.

Besides, the story isn't finished. What was past tense has become present tense again. We have now become part of the story again. It is no longer about what happened back then, but what will happen next. It is a story on the move, again being written by a new cast of characters—the 12 people sequestered in the back jury room of Courtroom 230. And that is the terrifying part of it now.

We are also part of it again. Until the jury makes a decision, we have to stay within 15 minutes of Room 230. We will be just hanging out—waiting— from 9 in the morning till 9:30 at night.

This takes the "exquisite art of waiting" to a whole new level that I'm not sure we are prepared for.

Come wait with us on the fourth floor. I have no idea how to live out this part of the story.

28

Deliberations were now well into their third day, prompting growing concern about whether or not the jury would even be able to reach a verdict. Each passing hour increased the possibility that jurors might be deadlocked. And if all 12 weren't ultimately able to agree, Justice Glenn Joyal would have no choice but to declare an automatic mistrial.

A hung jury was the worst case scenario for the Derksen family. The thought of having to go through another full trial, likely a year or two down the road, was unfathomable. The family was much more prepared to accept any verdict—even not guilty—than to have these past few weeks essentially count for nothing. They had come so far on this journey. It needed to end.

But there hadn't been a peep from the jury room since deliberations began. No questions, no requests for clarification on the law or to see or listen to exhibits. Nobody knew what the silence meant. But with the weekend looming, the clock was certainly ticking.

....

He had sat silently in the prisoner's dock, never uttering a word during his month-long trial. But it was more

than just Mark Grant's voice that jurors were deprived
of hearing. Grant's silence meant his dark criminal past
was kept secret from the people who were in the process
of deciding his fate. With jurors now sequestered, media
outlets were free to publish details about Grant that were
previously covered by a publication ban.

The *Winnipeg Free Press* ran a series of post-trial
stories, revealing the "similar fact evidence" that Grant's
lawyer had tried to call involving Patricia Wilson, the so-
called "girl in the boxcar" from 1985. Members of the
public also heard for the first time about the preliminary
hearing testimony of Tania Lachance, who had previously
claimed Grant confessed to Candace's murder in 1988.

The *Free Press* also revealed details about Grant's
extensive history with the criminal justice system, which
would have been revealed in court had he taken the witness stand to testify. The reports included details about
Grant's schizophrenia and painted a chilling picture of a
mind previously preoccupied with disturbing rape fantasies, lust for vulnerable teens, a hatred of women and
unwillingness to take any treatment.

Cliff and Wilma Derksen were passing the nervous
hours with family, friends and a flood of media interviews.
The entire city was waiting on edge for the verdict.

Wilma was adamant to anyone who asked that
the outcome was now of little consequence. "It doesn't
change anything," she said as jurors were well into their
second day of deliberations. "It's not only about him. It's
about us too."

Wilma said this was all about going through a process, and having peace in the knowledge that the trial had occurred. "We can't let the verdict override the whole experience. We can't let it take away what we've always focused on. We can't control the verdict. You can control what you choose to remember, what you believe in."

She expressed sympathy for the jurors, admitting their task wasn't an easy one. "Based on the science I think this is really difficult for a layperson to understand. I think it's a complicated case."

Many were asking about closure, a word Wilma said she doesn't like to use. "I think Candace never really left us. Candace has been a presence. She has been a part of our identity," she said. "I can't believe that after 26 years someone can seem so real."

Wilma called the trial "million-dollar therapy." "I think I've really been in a place of appreciation. We've lived with the mystery for 26 years. We didn't have any sense of what really happened. All of this has been wonderful. There's been this huge learning. 'Oh! That's what happened!' We're having it explained to us."

And she believes the city had benefitted from the experience as well. "It traumatized the community, the parents and the children. People developed fear traumas around this. Now there are some explanations and answers."

....

They got the call just after 8 p.m. with the news they'd been waiting to hear but feared would never come. The jury had a verdict. Crown attorney Brian Bell called Cliff and Wilma Derksen, who instantly felt a sense of relief. Their prayers had been answered. Their journey for justice was about to come to an end.

....

A hush had fallen over the packed courtroom. Mark Grant sat in the prisoner's box, his face obscured to all those in the gallery. The silence was broken every few seconds by the sound of his shackles clanging together.

Several sheriff's officers sat at either side. Crown attorneys Brian Bell and Mike Himmelman paced nervously. Defence lawyer Saul Simmonds was speaking quietly with his client.

It was just before 9 p.m. when Justice Glenn Joyal walked into the courtroom. Everyone quickly took their seats. Joyal announced that jurors had a verdict. He asked everyone in the gallery to keep their emotions in check, saying he wouldn't tolerate any outbursts. Anyone who thought they might have trouble keeping it together should wait outside. Nobody left.

The jury was brought in. There were serious looks on all their faces, signs of fatigue as well. At least one of the women appeared to be fighting tears. Joyal asked for the jury foreman to stand. One of the male jurors rose, a slip of paper in his hand. Joyal asked for him to read the verdict.

"We find Mark Grant not guilty of first-degree murder ... but guilty of second-degree murder," the foreman said.

There was no audible or visible reaction by anyone in the room.

Joyal repeated the verdict back and asked for confirmation. All 12 jurors agreed it was correct. One of the women was crying, while several others were clearly emotional as well. Joyal thanked them for their time, effort and dedication to the case. He then asked jurors to take a few minutes to return to their room and consider whether they had a recommendation for Grant's parole eligibility.

Grant now faced a mandatory life sentence with no chance of parole for at least 10 years. But Joyal had discretion to raise eligibility all the way up to 25 years if he felt it was warranted. It was standard procedure to ask a jury in a second-degree murder case if they had a view on the issue.

Jurors returned a few minutes later, announcing they didn't want to take any position on the issue. Joyal thanked them once again, and then repeated the standard final instructions to the jury. Those included a warning to never discuss the specifics of their deliberations. They were then dismissed and Joyal adjourned proceedings for a future sentencing date.

Once court was closed, the emotions which had been held in check began to flow. Cliff and Wilma Derksen embraced their family members and friends. Crown and defence lawyers exchanged handshakes as a sign of mutual respect.

The Derksens also thanked several of the police officers who were involved in the high-profile investigation and had rushed downtown on this cold winter's night to catch the verdict.

"I'm glad we could do this for you, that you put your trust in us," an emotional Det. Al Bradbury told Cliff.

Outside court, Cliff and Wilma spoke to the throng of media who were covering the case.

"I think the jury was tremendously courageous," said Wilma, wiping her eyes while clutching a fresh white rose in her hands. "It's a symbol of innocence, purity, love and fresh beginnings," she said of the flower.

Cliff was quick to thank police officers who were determined to solve the case, and the Crown prosecutors who made a convincing case to the jury. The family said they weren't disappointed jurors found Grant not guilty of the original charge of first-degree murder. They were just happy to have a verdict.

"The way this story has come together has completed us," said Wilma.

....

SATURDAY FEBRUARY 19, 2011

They gathered around the gravesite, about 30 family members and friends clutching white roses in their hands. "This is a recommitment to love, to forgiveness, to life," Wilma Derksen told those gathered inside Glen Eden cemetery. "We're going to live."

The Derksens had awakened in the morning and felt as if a weight had been lifted. And now they were surrounded by some of the most supportive and caring people in their lives to pay tribute to Candace. There were prayers, poetry readings, tears and even some laughter. The family passed around chocolates to all in attendance as a small token of their thanks. "Take one even if you hate chocolate," Cliff said with a smile.

Remarkably, there were also words of absolution and forgiveness for the man who had put Candace here. "It's not about letting go of accountability or justice," said Wilma. "Forgiveness allows us to get to justice in a better way."

At the end of the brief ceremony, everyone laid their rose on Candace's headstone. A new chapter in their lives was underway.

"I woke up this morning and I just felt different," said Wilma.

"It's like you don't have this hanging over your head anymore," said Cliff. "Like the bucket list is gone."

....

The abduction-slaying of Candace Derksen 26 years ago was a watershed event for Winnipeg. Parents held their children closer, Child Find was created, the term streetproofing was born and police re-examined their practices for searching for missing children. In the courtroom, however, none of that mattered. It was just another case bound by the rules of law and evidence.

The legal system has been criticized for setting the guilty free, but also for convicting the innocent. The principles of justice are not perfect and they are too often misunderstood and scorned by the general public, but they are based on centuries of precedent and trial and error.

The outcome of the five-week murder trial of Mark Edward Grant, then, is an opportunity to consider a few of the rules that affected the case for both the defence and the Crown.

The jury in a criminal trial is frequently in the dark on some issues. They might wonder, for example, if the accused is a person of bad character or if he or she has committed similar crimes in the past. They might also wonder why the accused does not take the stand to scream out his innocence, even though judges go to pains to explain defendants do not have to testify and jurors should not draw any conclusions from such silence.

In the Grant trial, there were many things the jurors did not hear. They were never told a case with similar facts happened within a year of the disappearance of Candace. A 12-year-old girl was tied up in a train car located near the Derksen home and abandoned by her abductor. At the time, police said the incident was eerily similar to the Derksen case. No one was ever arrested.

The defence was not allowed to tell the jury about the case, nor the fact Grant couldn't have been the culprit because he was in jail at the time. It might have raised reasonable doubt about Grant's guilt, but the problem was the victim today says the story was not true.

The judge ruled against admitting the story because it was unreliable and lacked credibility.

Similar-fact evidence can be allowed, but it must meet a high standard of relevance and probative value, a test the recanted abduction story failed to achieve, which doesn't mean it won't be a ground for appeal.

The Crown also had powerful evidence the jury did not hear, but it was the kind of evidence that is rarely allowed. The prosecution could have shown Grant had a record of sexual assault and a history of mental illness, that he was a very bad man, the very kind of man capable of abducting a young girl, tying her up and leaving her to die.

The prosecution did not even attempt to tell the jury all of that because it was inadmissible. That's because Grant's character was not on trial and evidence of his past conduct would have been overwhelmingly prejudicial, distracting the jury from considering only the facts linking him to Candace's abduction and death. It would have been different if Grant had taken the witness stand. Then his credibility would have been fair game.

The argument for admitting his record as evidence might be valid if his past crimes were identical to the Derksen case, but they were not. Telling the jury a defendant is a bad person is a prescription for a wrongful conviction.

Everyone is entitled to a fair trial and an appeal. But victims and their families are also entitled to know defendants have been convicted or acquitted on the basis of the highest standards of justice.

Tainted evidence and tainted verdicts affect them, too, particularly in the case of wrongful convictions, but also when verdicts are overturned because of critical errors made during the trial.

At this point, notwithstanding the appeal process, Wilma and Cliff Derksen can be comfortable with the idea that justice has been done, and that Candace can rest in peace.

—*WINNIPEG FREE PRESS* EDITORIAL

29

There were so many people to thank—loving family, supportive friends, caring neighbours and kind-hearted strangers who had joined them on their incredible journey. With the end finally in sight, Wilma Derksen had been struggling to find a way to thank everyone who had made an impact in their lives.

The result was something she was calling "Impact Dinner" in an invitation she extended through her personal blog.

> *As you probably already know, the sentencing of Mark Edward Grant was remanded to May 26, to be held at 10 in the morning in the Law Courts building—exact room to be determined. Even though we can never be certain, this time it looks as if the unexpected concerns were addressed and a decision will be made.*
>
> *I have mixed feeling about this date and what it means, so I am again trying to anticipate what we all might need.*
>
> *How do we fashion our own closure, not only to the day but to the entire process?*
>
> *When I was in Flin Flon, the women at the retreat wanted to know about our journey but also wanted*

to know about the person who had taken Candace's life. I was surprised and didn't understand it at the time, but I do now.

He is part of the ongoing story, and it isn't about excluding parts of the story but learning how to integrate them into our own. How do we tell this new story?

These days, the trial process actually gives victims an opportunity to submit a "victim impact statement." And we as a family have been continually asked if we are going to give our victim impact statement in court that day. We know there will be opportunity for us and for him to speak.

A victim impact statement is a written description of how a crime has affected you—the emotional, spiritual, financial and physical effects of the crime.

We need to let you know that we, as a family, have chosen not to give it in the courthouse for various reasons. We don't think it will actually make a difference to the court's decision, and we also have reason to believe that the victim impact statements can interfere with the actual justice-making process.

However, we do feel the actual process of writing down the impact of the crime is a healthy process, not only for ourselves, but also for friends and supporters who have been impacted.

So we are suggesting a "victim impact dinner" as something we can offer to you and our family.

On the evening of May 26, we will order in a catered meal (probably Homers—love their lemon *chicken)—and invite all of you who would like to come to our home for a "backyard dinner" 6 p.m. at our home, at which time we will read our victim impact statements.*

We know that we are not the only ones who are victimized by this murder so we would also like to invite you to write out your impact statement—if you are so inclined. For those of you who can't make it, feel free to write one and email it to us and we can read it. We will value and honour the stories.

In order to know how much chicken to order, we will need a RSVP."

. . . .

THURSDAY MAY 26, 2011

WITNESSING SENTENCING

"Would you meet with him?"

I don't know. I don't think I need to anymore. I'm not even sure I want to anymore.

Three years ago when I started this blog, I knew very little about the person who had murdered our daughter. All we knew was that "someone" had been charged with the murder. Now many of those initial questions have been answered.

Actually today is the day of sentencing. It's the oddest thing to be part of this process, to think of sentencing a life.

To tell you the truth, I really don't want to go to the law courts building today. I feel that personally I don't need to go. I believe that the judge, given the guilty verdict, will know what to do. He has enough information to sentence the murderer. He doesn't need us, and he doesn't need our words written out in a victim impact statement.

But when I asked someone whether I should go, they said, "Perhaps it is time for you to witness his life."

Whatever does that mean?

Apparently, bearing witness means to show by your presence that something is true. It is a human-to-human way of being by being attentive to the truth of someone's experiences. In other words, we all need to have witnesses to feel that we are alive, that we exist and that what is happening to us is real.

There have been many who have been there for us during this trial, validated us, and paying attention to our experience of it all. We felt supported by their presence. We began to depend on it. We are still depending on it. There are many who are coming to our dinner tonight and we are grateful for each one. There are many others who are thinking of us and praying for us. We feel it all. So we know the importance of being accompanied through a tough time.

Is our friend right? Is it now our turn to be that witness for someone else's life? Does this sentencing process need our presence and our attention to give it the importance it needs?

Do we have the capacity to be there for him, or will we still be there for us? Do we really want to

help him in his search for truth? Can we endure his
truth? Can he endure his truth?
  I don't know.

....

It was the day of reckoning for Mark Grant. And
Manitoba justice officials were going for the maximum
sentence allowed by law. In a fairly rare move, they wanted Justice Glenn Joyal to raise Grant's parole eligibility
all the way up to 25 years.

"This shocked the city of Winnipeg," Crown attorney
Brian Bell said near the beginning of his hour-long sub-
mission. "A young girl, from a good family, who never
made it home from school that day. It was completely random, therefore frightening to society at large." Bell spent
several moments reviewing the chilling circumstances of
Grant's crime. "Any reasonable member of society would
find Grant's actions sadistic, callous," he said.

Bell then provided extensive details about Grant's
past, which includes 23 previous convictions that had
already seen him spend more than 20 years behind bars.
He noted Grant had been diagnosed as a high risk to
reoffend, especially when he stopped taking antipsychotic medications to treat schizophrenia. Grant also had a
disturbing history of violent sexual fantasies, including
several he'd acted upon. He particularly enjoyed elements of pain, suffering and humiliation on his victims.
He told one probation officer. "All women are the same,
they deserve to be treated like dirt" while claiming he got
an "extra kick out of watching his victims squirm."

"He is an intensely troubled individual," said Bell. Grant was described as being anxious, depressed, introverted, mistrustful and of "below average level intelligence." "A lot of his anger is very primitive, uncontrolled," he said.

Defence lawyer Saul Simmonds had objected to some of the material being used against his client, saying much of it was based on summaries and opinions that might not be entirely accurate.

Sentencing had originally been scheduled for late April but had to be adjourned for further argument and discussion about what could be presented at the sentencing hearing. Joyal ultimately decided to give Bell plenty of leeway, ruling Grant's character and behaviour over the years were key factors when considering whether to raise parole eligibility.

One report stated Grant had an "inability to function in a pro-social environment in the community." Another suggested he hadn't been honest about much of his offending history and circumstances of his life. Several reports had concluded there was "no adequate community supervision that exists to protect citizens," said Bell.

Grant also reported having some "command hallucinations" when he stopped taking his antipsychotic medication in the past. He described symptoms including having voices "talking to him at night, leading him to believe he is the Devil," court was told.

Bell urged the judge not to give much weight to the fact Grant apparently experienced a traumatic, troubled upbringing. "You have to deal with Grant the way he is, not the way you wish he was," said Bell.

....

Saul Simmonds said this was not the time to try and "get even" with Mark Grant. He urged Joyal to only raise parole eligibility as high as 14 years. He said Grant wasn't given a fair shot at life, thanks to a history that included being abandoned by his mother, sexually, physically and emotionally abused by his father and then molested in a facility CFS sent him to as a teenager. "He was taunted, hurt and destroyed by the father," said Simmonds. He urged Joyal not to lash out at Grant out of a misguided sense of justice.

He said Grant functioned well in the community following his latest release from prison in 2004. He spent more than three years in the community without reoffending while embracing programming and treatment.

Simmonds said his client has started exploring his spiritual side, noting a nun who has been working with Grant behind bars was in court on this day for support. He also reminded Joyal that the jury clearly rejected first-degree murder. He said raising parole eligibility to 25 years would essentially be over-riding their second-degree verdict.

He also said the exact circumstances of the crime remained "far from clear" and that Grant was continuing to maintain his innocence. "We're left in somewhat of a quandary here," Simmonds said. But he thought the maximum sentence should be reserved for the "worst offender and the worst offence"—and Grant didn't qualify for either. Simmonds said there is no evidence Grant sexually assaulted Candace, or even physically injured her beyond the fact she was hog-tied.

"If there were true justice, Ms. Derksen would be returned to her family," said Simmonds.

....

Justice Glenn Joyal was ready with his decision. He wasted no time cutting to the chase—and hammering Mark Grant with the maximum penalty allowed by law. "This was a senseless and unspeakably cruel act. Uncertainty and dread eventually gave way to horror," said Joyal. He said there was no hesitation in raising parole eligibility to 25 years, based on the shocking nature of the notorious crime and Grant's terrible criminal record.

Joyal said jurors clearly found Grant had the state of mind required for murder when he abandoned a hog-tied Candace in freezing temperatures, thus causing her death. "These were circumstances that shocked and unsettled the city of Winnipeg," said Joyal. "He tied up and abandoned a little girl to be left to the cruelties of a Winnipeg winter."

Grant had no visible reaction to the sentence. Outside court, Cliff and Wilma Derksen admitted they took no joy in what had just occurred. "We grieve. This is just putting another life away, so that's hard. This doesn't bring Candace back," said Wilma.

Cliff described similar "mixed feelings." "Yes, he's paying for what he did, for bad decisions. But there's a difficulty in seeing a broken man, who's going to live in a prison system for at least 25 years."

Wilma said she wished Grant would have said a few words in court, rather than choose to remain silent when given an opportunity by the judge. "I think that's probably what's missing in all of this," she said. The family is open to eventually meeting with Grant behind bars, if he were willing. "Forgiveness is an ongoing process," Wilma said.

....

They had walked out of the courthouse shortly after 3:30 p.m., a feeling of hollow sadness and overwhelming grief washing over them. "We were sentencing a life away. I don't like seeing a human being suffer, contained and discarded," Wilma Derksen would say after the fact. They had spent a considerable amount of time speaking with reporters outside the downtown Winnipeg complex before going to their vehicle parked nearby.

Cliff and Wilma looked at each other and smiled. A genuine, heartfelt smile. They could both feel it. A sense of freedom, unlike anything they had ever experienced before.

"I want goldfish," Wilma said to her husband as they drove to their south Winnipeg home.

Cliff knew exactly what she was talking about. "Yes, let's go buy our goldfish," he said lovingly.

They stopped at their local pet store, an eye on the clock considering they were expecting a house full of company in short order. They were quickly met with disappointment. The goldfish tanks were nearly empty.

Moments later, a store clerk walked over with some good news. "Oh yes, there are a few goldfish that were dropped off. We're just trying to get rid of them," he said.

It was perfect. Absolutely perfect. Cliff and Wilma welcomed the opportunity to bring these rejected fish to their home. The three large, colourful fish would be a perfect fit for their backyard pond.

"Our guests will love them," Wilma said to her husband. In reality, they both knew the truth. This was about them. This was about Candace. This was about new life and fresh beginnings. This was about hope.

Wilma went straight to the pond when they got home. The fish quickly took to their new home, darting underneath several large rocks. They were out of sight. But for Wilma, they certainly weren't out of mind.

30

Their guests began arriving on time, right around 6 p.m. They were greeted with a smiles, hugs and handshakes from Cliff and Wilma and their daughter, Odia. It was a cool evening, especially for late May. Temperatures were expected to drop near freezing. Chairs had been set up in a circle inside their gazebo. Guests quickly filled in, grabbing a drink, some chicken and salads that had been catered from their favourite restaurant. It was nearly 7 p.m. when Cliff and Wilma spoke to the group. It was time to get started.

Wilma explained how thrilled she was to see many friends, some old, many new, on such an important day in their lives. She suggested they go around the circle, each person taking a few moments to describe who they were and what had brought them there.

This was for the benefit of the entire group, some 50 people strong, who certainly did not all know each other but had come together on this night for a common purpose. Wilma also wanted to know what they were thinking after such a monumental event, the sentencing of Candace's killer. Finally, she asked everyone to provide a single word, or two perhaps, that best summarized their thoughts and feelings.

It was going to be an emotional evening.

....

"There is no jubilation in the moment," their first guest began. Gerry Michalski was a long-time family friend who also happened to be their pastor. He expressed the deep hurt and anger he felt at hearing about Mark Grant's twisted past for the first time in court earlier that day. He told the gathering he felt "dirty" upon hearing of Grant's hatred towards women.

"My word, or phrase, would be 'Beauty out of ashes'," he concluded. The phrase was from Isaiah, and Wilma thought it was the perfect start to their sharing circle.

Michalski's wife was next. She described the evening as a celebration of "the end of a chapter." And certainly the beginning of a new one.

Harold Jantz had known the Derksen family for many years and was one of the organizers of the original search party for Candace. He spoke to the group about the impact this case had on the city and province. "The disappearance of Candace generated a great deal of public interest and concern because something so random had seldom happened in the experience of most people of our city. When it was learned that she had been murdered, virtually everyone in our city and many across the country knew about it. The various media, daily papers, radio and television played a huge part in telling your story. It became an occasion even at that time to make a powerful Christian statement by the way you folks responded," Jantz told the Derksens.

"You folks have blessed us in several ways through this great tragedy. In the first place, you have allowed many others to observe you as you dealt with what happened to Candace. That openness has not only aided your own healing, it has helped others to heal from situations that they have had to deal with. Furthermore, you have shown God's grace at work in you. So much good has come out of this terrible experience, when it could have destroyed you and left only bitterness in its wake. Many others have been affected for the good by that grace at work in you."

Jantz went on to explain how he had attended an evening church service at St. Benedict's Table the previous Sunday when he ran into Brian Bell, the lead Crown prosecutor on the case. "He was part of the service and participated in the communion service. He is a Christian man. What a thrill to discover that," said Jantz. "I spoke to him briefly after the service and thanked him for his good work in the trial. I was especially grateful to think that a person with a Christian conscience should have been presenting the case against the accused. That would not be a guarantee that justice was being done, but it should be an encouragement to a search for the truth in this matter. In my estimation, nothing that he did throughout the trial would have undermined what he might have claimed as a Christian."

They continued around the room. One woman described her feelings of the day as "shock and awe." Another spoke about a strong feeling of bonding she had experienced throughout the ordeal, a coming together of "family." Another woman used the term "connecting."

"Generosity," said Lisa Phommarath, another good friend of the family. "My thoughts were just how generously you gave of your time during your own hearing and trial. And Cliff, as well."

"Exhale," said Misty Blake-Knox.

Brian Campbell called the evening a "new beginning." He described Cliff and Wilma as "amazing."

"Once in a blue moon, justice happens," said Bernie Bowman.

Horst Peters and his wife, Heidi, took turns expressing their support and love for the Derksens.

"Providing support is one of the easiest things friends can do and we're very happy to do that," said Horst. He used the word "conflicted" to summarize the ordeal, and then explained in eloquent fashion what he meant.

"I have been involved in mental health for more than 20 years—as a patient, a respite worker, an educator and advocate. Much of my work was centered around advocating for better services for people with mental disorders, for more comprehensive services, more opportunities for people to participate fully in our communities, and to reduce the stigma that impacts people living with mental disorders.

"Every time I read or hear a news report that mentions the fact that a perpetrator of a crime has a mental disorder, I cringe. I wonder what role, if any, the disorder played in the criminal act. If it wasn't a contributing factor, I wonder why that information was included. Was it just another statement perpetuating the myth that people with mental disorders, especially schizophrenia and bipolar disorder, are dangerous, violent, and liable to hurt or possibly kill someone at any time. I wonder what the whole story is.

"When I read that Mark Grant had been diagnosed with schizophrenia I cringed again. I wrestled with the question of whether or not I could or even would advocate for Mark especially because I know some of the impact his actions have had on you, your family and many friends. I really questioned whether his illness was a factor in his abduction, torture and murder of Candace. Nothing I had read or heard before and after the trial indicated to me that the schizophrenia played a role in his actions. Although illnesses such as schizophrenia are the primary factor in tragic and horrific occurrences, I don't see that in Mark's abduction and killing of Candace. All I see is that a man chose to act in an evil and twisted way. Illness is not an excuse for intentional bad choices and evil behaviour.

"I hurt for your loss and pain, I hurt for Candace's loss of life, I hurt for the tragedy of Mark Grant's life, and I am angered that the publication of his diagnosis will perpetuate the stigma of the violent, crazy, dangerous person with an illness like schizophrenia. The reality is that people with schizophrenia and other mental disorders are far more likely to be victims than perpetrators.

"I am glad justice has been served. I am glad this chapter has ended for you."

....

Richard Hyslop first met Cliff Derksen in July of 1985, six months after the disappearance and death of his daughter. At the time, he was a 19-year-old rookie counsellor at Camp Arnes. Cliff would have been 40 and was director of the camp's summer programs.

Hyslop initially knew very little about Candace's case. He was a student living in Three Hills Alberta who had only heard a few details in passing. But he would grow to understand the enormous impact the crime took on so many people while at the same time developing a strong friendship with the Derksens.

He stood in front of the group and shared his very powerful story. "In the middle of August 1985, I had opportunity to witness another completely different, otherwise hidden part to Cliff's personality," he began.

"Cliff had been asked to share with our camp's young summer staff the experience of the loss of his daughter. Though normally quick to find words, that night Cliff struggled to find words to express himself. Though normally light-hearted in presentation, I can still vividly recall the pained expression on Cliff's face that night. Even a young man like myself could instantly recognize that a completely broken man was standing before me, a man suffering from much suppressed emotional pain.

"The only words I can now recall was Cliff saying: 'I wish I was dead. Then I could be with Candace again.' I instinctively knew he had thought about what he he'd just said and was being serious, not over-dramatic.

"I wondered if Cliff might be suicidal."

In fact, Hyslop would later learn that both Cliff and Wilma had experienced suicidal thoughts throughout the years.

He continued: "My instinctive thought at that moment in 1985 was: 'Buddy, you need to get a grip on reality and see all the beauty around us.' For me, that beauty was all the young available female camp staff I observed around me. I now realize that a married man of 40 wouldn't be looking at that beauty in the same manner.

"My initial instinctive thought was quickly followed up by this second thought: 'Rick, this is a sacred moment here. You have no idea what this man is talking about, but need to bottle this experience. It might someday make more sense to you. While I couldn't then grasp Cliff's pain, I could grasp that he was exposing his inner-most thoughts, putting himself in a vulnerable position. As a young man, I could appreciate the courage it took to do that. I was honoured and humbled by Cliff's gesture. I think that's why I decided to treasure the moment as sacred."

Hyslop also recalled details of a private late night conversation he and Cliff once had at Camp Arnes. "Cliff shared with me these words of wisdom: 'When we suffer something hugely traumatic and unjust, the experience stays with us for our entire life. Forgiveness concerning that traumatic injustice becomes a lifelong process. We have to continually choose forgiveness over and over and over, as we move through the various stages of life, and continually re-examine our past experiences and our continually evolving perspective on those experiences. It's NOT a one-time for all-time deal.'

"Those words meant a lot to me then and now. I suffered a difficult childhood with an abusive father. Having said that: I suspect Mark Edward Grant's father was much more abusive than mine. Perhaps more importantly, I had many other important supportive adults in my life—including a mother, grandparents, aunts and uncles—something I suspect Grant didn't have. Nevertheless, I did suffer considerable abuse as a child.

"When Cliff talked to me about forgiveness so many years ago, it was in the context of talking about my relationship with my father. About 18 months after getting away from my father's home and abuse, as a 15 year-old, I was able to forgive my father for the things he had done to me as a child.

"I say all that to say Cliff was so right when he recognized so long ago that the choice to 'forgive' Candace's killer would be a lifelong journey of numerous choices. And I believe he has done remarkably well with that journey! Better than most would do. Better than I would do."

Hyslop now fast-forwarded his story to more present time, recalling the day he learned Candace's killer had finally been arrested.

"Over twenty years later, in May of 2007, I found myself alone at a truck stop in Pennsylvania. By this time, I was a long distance truck driver, at the end of a long but routine day. As was my daily custom, I called home to my wife, who was living in Moncton, New Brunswick, before settling down for the night in my truck bunk. It was through her that I learned of the arrest of Mark Edward Grant.

"My initial reaction was shock. Like most, I had given up hope that Candace's killer would ever be found. With the news dominating my thoughts, I returned to my truck and lay down in my truck's bunk. I was alone and lonely as I let the news sink into my thoughts. My shock quickly gave way to tears.

"The tears took me by surprise. I thought I should be filled with joy at the news the mystery of Candace's killer was being solved. As I wondered why I was crying at what I thought should be a joyous moment, I began to cry even harder, eventually sobbing uncontrollably.

"I thought maybe I was mourning Candace's death, but then remembered I had never met Candace, let alone grown attached to her. Wilma has since suggested that my tears were due to my attachment to Cliff and her. Though I think there's some truth to that explanation, there's a deeper explanation.

"As I pondered the cause of my sudden deep sorrow, I realized my oldest daughter was then the same age as Candace when she died, and her younger sister the same age as Candace's younger sister, Odia.

"My thoughts instantly went back to Cliff's now ancient words: 'I wish I was dead.' That's when I began to sob uncontrollably. The thought of how I'd feel if someone were to do to my 13-year-old daughter what had been done to Candace overwhelmed me. Actually, I couldn't sustain that thought. It was unbearable. I was no longer thinking like a childless 19-year-old. Cliff's pain now made perfect rational sense to me. Now I'm left to wonder how he maintained his sanity.

"The only rational answer I have to that question is that he had to, for the sake of his two surviving children. My daughters are now 17 and 13. Parenting is tough, even under the best of circumstances. I've had opportunity to engage both Odia and Syras as adults. They are intelligent, compassionate human beings and productive citizens. As a father myself, I would now say to Cliff: 'Well done good and faithful father. May your just reward be an eventual joyous reunion with Candace.'"

31

Darkness had begun to fall and there was a chill in the air. Nobody seemed to mind. Everyone took a short break to stretch, refill their glasses and grab some blankets.

Chris Rutkowski had guests reaching for a dictionary when he used the term "revenant" to describe his thoughts. "The word itself means 'one who returns' and it also means 'one who returns after a long absence'. In some definitions, however, the word implies something much more; it refers to a soul or spirit who has come back to complete some unfinished business or for carrying a message to those alive on Earth. In some ways, Candace did indeed come back for closure and to give comfort to her family and friends that night. There was something left undone: grieving with her mother and father, bringing justice, and giving permission to 'go on'," said Rutkowski.

His wife, Donna, used the word "family" to summarize her feelings.

Irene Froese had only met the Derksen family after Candace's killing. She had worked at a grocery store on Henderson Highway in Winnipeg which employed several girls from Candace's school. She told the gathering how the case had always weighed heavily on her mind.

"We saw the girls and the strain they were under. We also had three daughters, and could never imagine anything like that happening to us," said Froese. She used the word "awesome" to end her remarks. "It seemed to be so suitable for the way Judge Joyal made the case, and he seemed to sum up everything that he had held in during all those weeks of the trial. I was just so moved and I felt so grateful for your family, that you got what you deserved. Hope life will get more settled for you all now. I will always remember it all," she said.

Another long-time friend said it was inspiring to see how the family had survived their ordeal. "So much good has come out of this terrible experience. It could have destroyed you and left only bitterness in its wake. Many others have been affected for good by the grace at work in you," she said.

Heidi Friesen had many guests fighting back tears as she spoke about the weekend sleepover with Candace that never happened. She told the gathering how she'd met Candace at the age of 11 and they quickly became best friends.

And how now, on the verge of turning 40, she still felt a deep connection to Candace. "My best friend is forever 13 years old," she said.

....

The image of Candace Derksen's laughing, smiling face was forever frozen into Dave Wiebe's memory. So, too, were the circumstances of their final moments together on that school playground.

"I met Candace at camp and was very attracted to how full of life she was," Wiebe told the backyard gathering. "She was great to be around, always smiling and just had a way to make you feel good to be around her." Wiebe proposed a toast, asking everyone to consider the incredible impact Candace had on their lives.

"She blessed us all with her positive attitude and just the way she loved life to the fullest. People were clearly important to Candace and she was just someone you wanted to be around. So, Candace, for all the smiles you shared, for the infectious way you loved life, and for all that you were during your short time with us I ask us all to raise you glass in this toast for Candace."

Wiebe then described how their short time together had left such a lasting impression. "I got to know Candace at Camp Arnes and felt she was someone special right from the first time I met her. I remember when school started and I saw her there I couldn't believe it. I walked up to her and asked her how old she was and was shocked to hear her say 13 as I figured she was my age, 15. Even though only two years difference she was in grade 7 and I was in grade 11. Our class schedule was much different from each other so we did not meet very often but every chance I could I would make a point to say hi or, on one occasion, sit beside her on the bleachers during some sporting event in the gym.

"She was always so happy to see me and I was always glad to see her. On the day that she went missing I actually saw her twice and included her in a snowball fight that was going on with my friends. I last saw Candace in the parking lot as she was leaving school and would have loved to drive her or even walk her home but unfortunately I had driver's education right away and had to settle for just saying goodbye.

"She was one of very few who called me David and as I said goodbye she said 'Goodbye David'. After Drivers Ed I had choir practice and once that was over I noticed a lady walking toward me. She asked me if I was David Wiebe and I said 'Yes' and then she introduced herself as Wilma Derksen, Candace's mom. Little did I know that that day would literally change me forever.

"I went from concern for Candace to being questioned from police to pleading with God to bring Candace back to grieving her death to 23 years after taking a polygraph and giving my DNA to eliminate me as a 'person of interest' as the police called it, to sitting in court for five weeks witnessing first hand as to how our justice system works.

"So this story has been a part of my life for many years and that is why there is no way I couldn't be a part of meeting with you all here tonight. I am thankful to have this moment to hear all of your stories. Thanks so much to Cliff and Wilma or always welcoming me in their home. I love them like family and will do whatever I can to help them whenever and however I can."

....

Daile Unruh-Peters recalled the monumental impact Candace's case had on the community—and how the

Derksens strength and courage had guided her through her own difficult times in life.

"I remember the time when Candace disappeared and then her body was discovered. I was living in Winnipeg and I remember the complete shock that the community felt. This did not happen in Winnipeg. There was a loss of innocence and in many ways Winnipeg was never the same. In a sense the community froze in the same way that Candace froze. Perhaps now, with this verdict and sentencing, the community at large can receive some type of closure, some type of thawing of its soul," she said.

"I met Cliff and Wilma through the ministry of listening at Soul Sanctuary, and had no idea who they were until one day they came to our meeting and began the morning by telling us that they were not sure they could make it through the morning because that week they had received news that an arrest was going to be made in the 25-year-old, unsolved murder of their daughter Candace. And then, they continued on to teach us how to listen, how to create an environment in which people can be heard, and in being heard, not feel so alone.

"A couple of years later as I was trying to bring some closure to an abusive marriage and the subsequent death of my then husband, it was actually our pastor who suggested that I talk with Wilma as a way of finding closure. She was very pivotal in working with me to achieve closure, to understand that forgiveness is an ongoing process, to learning to live acknowledging both the trauma of my experiences with him yet continuing to choose to move forward, to have the courage to build a new life.

"Somehow you have had the courage and faith to determine that every day since this horrible tragedy began you would continue to believe that God will turn this into something good. You have lived that out through the days when there were no answers to what happened to Candace, and you have lived that out through the trial and sentencing, through the days when you spoke of forgiveness, and even tonight as you have expressed that there is no pleasure for you in the sentencing of a man to life in prison, that your hearts ache for the experiences that Mark Edward Grant endured and the choices he made as a means of dealing with his rage and grief.

"On many days when you didn't feel as if you could, or should, it seems to me that the two of you deliberately chose to cling to faith in a God who would use this for good, despite the evil that Mark Edward Grant so clearly intended. I know that I have been blessed by and benefitted from your determination to say 'God, we will choose to believe that you can use for good what Mark Edward Grant intended for evil' in the midst of, and in spite of, your grief and loss. I think many here tonight have benefitted as well."

....

Among the crowd on this night sat three people who had only just met the Derksen family—but who had played a pivotal role in the case. All three had sat on the jury which convicted Mark Grant of murder. They had come to the sentencing hearing for Grant, seeking closure to a case that had deeply impacted them and a chance meeting in the hallway with Cliff and Wilma had led to an open invitation to drop by their home for a visit. And while the jurors were forever prohibited from speaking about their deliberations, there was nothing to stop them from post-trial socializing.

The first juror to speak was a young man who told the group he had grown up in Ireland, only to marry a Canadian woman and become a landed immigrant. He discussed being 5,000 miles away when Candace was killed and knowing absolutely nothing about the case until the trial began. But he described being haunted by the chilling facts, overwhelmed at his responsibility and grateful for the opportunity provided by the Derksens to share in this special night.

The second juror was a young woman who had grown up in North Kildonan and was close to Candace's age at the time she vanished. The woman—who had been deemed impartial during jury selection and accepted by Crown and defence lawyers—said she was deeply moved at the strength and courage shown by the Derksens throughout their ordeal.

The third juror, another young woman, fought back tears as she discussed the impact this case had on her. She described how she struggled to get through each day of the trial, her anxiety and depression becoming almost too much to handle.

"After the first day of court walking to my car, I got in my car, burst into tears, called my husband and said 'I don't know if I can do this'. Was it going to be like this every day, I thought, with the pictures, all of the witnesses, and having to look at that person in the prisoner's box every day that has committed an unspeakable horrific crime? Was I naive in thinking that somehow it would be different? I didn't know. After a week of getting acquainted with my new friends and what felt like was a new way of life, it was getting harder, not easier, as somehow I thought it might. I found my depression creeping back quickly, my anxiety levels heightened and my obsessive and worrisome thoughts were there constantly," the woman told the gathering.

A noticeable hush had fallen over the group.

"As the trial continued, I started paying more attention to the people in the gallery," she continued. "Then it hit me, here I am worrying if I could get through this trial and here was the Derksen family who had lived this horrific nightmare for over 26 years. I felt so silly. A thought overwhelmed me, was there another reason that I'm on this jury, other than to bring justice? Could it be to help me within, to learn to deal with my own issues? I guess I would have to wait and see.

"After the trial was over, I was an emotional wreck. I was so obsessed with reading, listening and watching everything surrounded with the trial, over and over again. I just couldn't let it go. Being included and being able to talk with all of you about the trial has definitely helped to bring some closure to this experience. I am absolutely grateful that I was selected and able to help bring justice for your beautiful Candace and for your family. It has been an honour to be able to talk and start to get to know all of you."

....

They had finished going around the yard. Every single guest had spoken about what had brought them there. All that was left was to hear from Cliff and Wilma. But before they shared their thoughts, the family brought out several bottles of Dr. Zenzen, a sparkling wine accented with tiny gold flecks.

They popped the bottles and filled dozens of beautiful flutes which were distributed to the group. Everyone gathered in a circle, holding their drinks out and proposing a series of toasts.

"To Candace," said one guest.

"To old and new friends," said another.

"To love," added a third.

32

Cliff and Wilma Derksen walked to the centre of the gaze-bo, now illuminated by a string of lights against the night sky. This was the moment they had been waiting for. Both had struggled the write their words, choosing each one so very carefully. And now they were ready to share their deepest thoughts with the people who had helped them through their darkest hours.

....

Cliff began with a Bible verse, reading from Psalms 27:1. "The Lord is my light and my salvation…"

He then took his guests on a journey through his humble beginnings—growing up on a farm during simpler times when he still rode a horse to school, knowing the value of an honest day of work, and having church and family as the backbone of one's community.

Cliff described graduating high school and continuing his studies at Bethany Bible School where he met Wilma, knowing immediately he had met his soulmate. A beautiful wedding eventually followed. And then came the greatest gift a man could ask for. The birth of his daughter, Candace.

Cliff recalled memories of Candace, who started walking at seven months with legs so short her diaper almost dragged on the ground. He described teaching Candace to ride a bike, her love of swimming, which they did as a family, and their constant morning fight over white socks. "She liked mine because they stayed whiter than hers," Cliff said to much laughter.

His voice began to choke as he continued. "She was turning into a loving, caring woman with a multitude of friends ... and a number of very close and faithful friends," he said.

Cliff recalled the horrific night Candace vanished, how he ventured out into the frigid darkness in a desperate search down snowy streets and icy back alleys, all the while checking dumpsters and peering between sheds and buildings.

He described the tears which fell from his eyes, freezing to his cheeks, as he unleashed a primeval cry. "'Where is she? Why Candace? Why?...' The night felt cold and unresponsive, not giving up its secrets," he said.

Cliff discussed the horror of learning her body had been found, the pressure to find the person who had taken her and the growing suspicion which was falling upon him and hovered around the family. "It was understandable, since over 95% of all abductors are family members or known to the family. Who would have thought it was a stranger who had taken her?" Cliff said.

He described how the stress took its toll, his world starting to fall apart slowly but surely until he hit the bottom rung ten years later. His anger had become a problem. "Put to the ultimate test, I had to change. If

I couldn't change my life, I had to change my heart," said Cliff.

Cliff said he reached out in a new way to his faith in God. He started in anguish to memorize the book of Jonah. He started to heal. Cliff told guests how he'd just found equilibrium and a new purpose in his life with a new business venture when Mark Grant was arrested and charged with murdering his daughter. And yet, instead of anger he found himself feeling compassion for this unknown killer.

"Because I have experienced the north wind, I have compassion for those who are in trouble. Grant is in trouble. Because I have been forgiven, I can forgive. I pray that the consequences of his actions will bring him to know God in a personal way," said Cliff.

"Paralleling the entire horrific experience have been the amazing incidences of love and help. There were people who arrived at the right moment in my life with words of wisdom. God's guidance was visible to me. There were also amazing moments of prayer with the children, moments when the court became holy ground, and that final moment when it felt that truth had won. I finally knew what had happened and who had done it."

Cliff concluded his emotional speech by thanking everyone for coming to their special night.

"Thank you to you, our friends, who attended the trial, wrote cards, emails, visited us, gave us chocolate and more chocolate, phoned us, prayed for us and waited with us during the deliberation. You loved us in so many ways that we will never be able to repay you. Thank you."

....

Now it was Wilma's turn. She had sat in her office the previous evening, staring at the blank computer screen in front of her. She had tried to imagine someone being sentenced, to be given a set number of years imposed on them. And she had started to cry. Wilma imagined there couldn't be anything worse in life, an unbearable existence to be confined to a small, likely segregated cell year after year. She didn't know how the human spirit could endure it.

Wilma gave up on trying to complete her statement, returning to it earlier in the morning. But her struggle to find the right words had continued. Now somewhat finished, Wilma warned her friends they were about to hear an "unprocessed" statement. But it was coming straight from her heart.

"I grieve for the man who threw his life away and chose to hurt others as he was hurt," she began. "There are many who have been hurt like him who choose something else, a different way to deal with their pain, so I do not feel he had no choice but to act out his anger in this way. I place the responsibility of his actions on him.

"But by believing in choice and responsibility, which sounds harsh and condemning, it also means I believe in the ongoing opportunity to change, to choose something different, and to step out of his self-destructive behaviour into something life-giving. I know it is hard to change, especially as we get older, so I'm not holding my breath, but I will always wait for the change.

"I know that he was a charming person back then who could mesmerize the young with his bad boy/good boy personality. He must have been very exciting and resourceful to do what he did. I grieve all that misplaced charm.

"I grieve for Candace who is the real victim in all of this. Even though I can't speak for her …. I can tell you that I grieve her loss. She was my daughter, a lovely daughter, and there really are no words to describe the pain and the loss. I grieve that she wasn't able to live and love. I grieve that she was denied the beauty she sought. I grieve mostly that she died in the presence of someone who wanted to hurt her and hated her. I grieve for her loneliness that night, for her powerlessness, for her pain, and for her desperation. I grieve for her cry for help and that no one came to save her…. I grieve for that little girl, so innocent, so loving, so full of fun.

"I grieve for the young woman I was back then, who was so confused, so hurt, so vulnerable, and who tried to be so brave. I grieve for her sorrow. She made so many mistakes, and yet she tried so hard. I grieve those moments when she had to stifle her anger, her tears … and in spite of the pain kept on walking for her children and for her husband.

"I grieve for my husband who suffered more than anyone knows, I think more than he even knows. I grieve for his pain when all of the suspicion closed in on him and nearly suffocated him—and me.

"I grieve for my children who were neglected and threatened by a force too strong for them. How young they were when this all happened. They were too young to even have the words to express their pain, yet valiantly stepped up to the plate.

"I grieve for Candace's friends who were caught in a story that threatened to define them for the rest of their lives. I feel so guilty that they connected with us at the worst moment and then endured all of it with us.

"I grieve for her peers, an entire generation, who were sentenced to a life of fear, confined to their houses when they should have been set free, afraid of strangers when they should have been given permission to love.

"I grieve for a past that was so cruelly disrupted and suspended. We lost so much that day she died. We will never have enough words to describe it.

"But tonight, I also need to say that I feel blessed.

"I am grateful that Candace's memory is still vivid and strong. I am grateful that I could feel her presence in the courtroom and at the grave. I am grateful for the white roses I received, which in their beauty can symbolize my oldest daughter and her loveliness.

"I am so grateful to have been able to attend this trial, to have the opportunity to find out the answers to what happened that day. I am grateful that the truth has truly set us free—and that we could feel the air again under our wings. I am grateful that we can still feel. We aren't numb … we can feel. We can feel the joy, the pain, the sadness, the despair and the hope.

"I am grateful for the criminal justice system that does believe in process … for everyone who participated in this long and arduous process and solving the mystery. I am grateful for every police officer who helped in the case, for those who came to our door that first night and answered our cry for help, for the first investigators of missing persons, for the second wave of officers who investigated the crime scene, and for the countless others who worked on the case that got colder and colder with time. I am forever indebted to those who dusted off the files and looked at it again with new eyes and applied the new DNA learnings to it. I am amazed at the thoroughness of the Crown counsel, the judge and all of the staff at the Law Courts building who were so kind to us and our friends. We felt so cared for.

"I am grateful to the defence … who made us smile, who gave a valiant defence, who asked all the right questions. His relentless probing helped us believe in the validity of the guilty verdict. We had the assurance that it had been tested.

"I am grateful that we could do this all with our children and their spouses and that it united us rather than tore us apart. I am so proud of them all. I am grateful that at the most unbearable moment, we were one as a family and we could all stand on holy ground together. They are incredibly strong and wonderful … each one gifted in their own way.

"I am grateful for Candace's friends, who continue to live her legacy in their love for her. I am grateful that they too were healed and freed to some degree during this trial.

"I am grateful to all of our supporters. I am grateful that you didn't give up on us as a family and stayed connected.

"I am grateful for all of you here tonight. Each one of you brings something to my soul. I need a lot of attention it seems, and each one of you in your own way does something.

"It doesn't have to be much—it is often just that hint of a smile, that one word, that touch and that reassurance of your hug and presence that comforts me. You have no idea how important it is to me. I am by nature a lonely person. There is a part of me that huddles at the bottom of my soul—always feeling abandoned, who could have been so easily destroyed by this all … you kept her alive, and I am so grateful.

"I am grateful for my dear husband who never blamed me for not picking Candace up—who loved me enough never to say those words. Because he knew he had the power to save or destroy me.

"I am grateful that he has become stronger through this all.

"I could go on and on in my gratitude. There have been many during the twenty-six years of not knowing who accompanied us and continued to encourage us. There were old Bible School friends, church friends, neighbours, colleagues and even strangers, who just walked alongside us in the most sensitive and healing ways. They kept us afloat.

"I am grateful to a God who can work miracles, who remains mysterious, unfathomable, untouchable, and yet so close. A God who has shown us love, who has kept his promise to help us turn it into good, and who continues to show up. I have to admit there were times when I doubted it—and probably will again, but right now, my heart is overflowing with gratitude that he didn't walk away on us.

"What about the future?

"I want to remain open.

"I want to continue to be open to all of what my life has to offer. I want to keep learning, being challenged, to be open to the pain of living, open to the surprises, open to the toughness of life, the tiredness and the mundane. All of it.

"I want to keep my eyes wide open to the opportunities in life. I want to risk, dare new things, and walk where angels fear to tread.

"I want to stay loving. I am being challenged right now by the St. Leonard's project. I don't understand why I am doing what I'm doing or what brought me here to this point at this time, but it feels as if God isn't finished with me yet.

"I just pray for continued courage to face it all.

"And I want to continue to pray for Mark Edward Grant. I don't want to be his jailor or his mother, friend or anything like that. I just want to pray for him ... that he will someday regain the flame of God in him and know that he is loved.

"I want to stay in the pursuit of words. I don't want to give up the chase.

"Again, I thank you for coming tonight to this 'Impact Dinner'. Candace was right. Friends are friends forever. She is now an angel, at least in spirit, hovering very close.

"It's love that takes us through."

EPILOGUE

Mark Grant wasted little time trying to have his conviction and maximum sentence overturned. Documents were filed in early June 2011, asking the Manitoba Court of Appeal to order a new trial.

Defence lawyer Saul Simmonds cited 18 alleged errors made by Justice Glenn Joyal, who had since been promoted to Chief Justice of the Manitoba Court of Queen's Bench. They included Joyal's refusal to allow jurors to hear from Patricia Wilson, the so-called "girl in the boxcar" who dramatically changed her story during the pre-trial motion. Simmonds claimed his client was deprived of a fair hearing because Wilson was muzzled. Simmonds also claimed jurors should not have been allowed to hear any details of the 23-minute interview Grant had with police investigators shortly after Candace Derksen's disappearance.

Menno Zacharias had testified how Grant became a person of interest after his then-girlfriend, Audrey Fontaine, claimed she had seen Candace after she vanished. Grant—who was in custody at the Remand Centre at the time—told officers he didn't know the 13-year-old missing girl but admitted he had dyed his hair before his arrest. He also admitted to spending a few nights with Fontaine in the underground inspection pit in the

CPR Weston rail yards, about six kilometres from where Candace was found. Simmonds was concerned the details about Grant being in custody unfairly painted him as a "bad guy" in the eyes of the jury.

Simmonds also took issue with some of the opinion evidence the Crown was allowed to put to jurors from their forensic experts who testified. Simmonds had tried to suppress much of that evidence but was overruled by Joyal.

In the event his second-degree murder conviction appeal failed, Grant's "Plan B" involved arguing that his sentence was "unduly harsh" and should be reduced. Simmonds claimed there weren't sufficient grounds to raise parole eligibility to 25 years, which is the mandatory sentence for a first-degree murder conviction. Simmonds noted the jury acquitted Grant of that charge, yet he was then sentenced as if he'd been found guilty as charged.

The Crown took the position no mistakes were made and both conviction and sentence should stand. They planned to argue it was a rock-solid case built on indisputable scientific evidence. A three-justice panel of the Appeal Court was expected to hear arguments in either late 2011 or early 2012.

....

THE ENCOUNTER
By Wilma Derksen, Thursday June 2, 2011
"Would you meet with him?"

I have met with him. I did get all the questions answered that I needed. I have no need to meet with him further.

I think there is speculation that I want to meet with him.

When I was asked by the reporters at the front doors of the Law Courts building right after the sentencing if I would meet with him, I said if I did "it would have to begin with integrity and end with integrity."

What I meant was that as long as he is denying any involvement in the murder of our daughter, we really have nothing to talk about. We aren't going to get together to talk about the weather. That wouldn't be helpful. And I'm not going to try and convince him of the impact of the murder if he denies ever having done it. I can't even help him with something he didn't do. We have no meeting place.

They then asked if I hoped for an apology or change of heart. Would I meet with him if there was? I again used the word integrity. It really is the only word. I don't want an apology. I don't want change. I just want honesty and truth.

It is always a difficult journey into one's own truth. But I will not meet with him until I am convinced that it will be about truth and that he has embarked on that journey. He doesn't have to change or apologize; I can begin the conversation without that. But I can't begin a conversation without truth.

So in the language of the Room 230, I want to "be perfectly clear" that I am no longer seeking an opportunity to meet with Grant. We both had our day in court.

If the preliminary hearing and the five-week trial didn't convince him that denial no longer works, my feeble words will make no difference to him.

I also don't believe he has any need of me or my friends. From what I can gather, he has had ample opportunity to access love from many communities. I know he has attended good church programs. As far as I can tell he has made his choices in full awareness.

I also believe that as long as he is in denial, our family will continue to be vulnerable to his hate and manipulation. The reason he is serving a life sentence in prison is to protect people like us and other unsuspecting people in society from his potential predatory nature.

I can rest peacefully knowing there are professional people to look after him, and that they will continue to look after him with kindness and love.

The other question I often hear is: Will he change? I believe everyone has choices and everyone can change. But when someone has lived out their negativity for so long, it is much harder to change.

However I will not give up hope. If he should suddenly choose truth, begin to tell the true story, and he asked for us, I would consider meeting him. I do believe that all walls need to have gates, doors and windows.

But until then I have no further interest in the question. It is out of my hands.

Strangely enough, I do feel now I can fully forgive him. I can let it go, pray for him, bless him, and even support his stay in prison with our taxes willingly.

However I suspect the issues surrounding the murder will never leave us. We are always facing the battle of good and evil in the world and in ourselves. We will continue to collide with him symbolically in so many different ways … probably every day.

In that way it will never be over.